S0-CFY-827

Old Testament
Commentary Survey

Old Testament Commentary Survey

Third Edition

Tremper Longman III

 Baker Academic

A Division of Baker Book House Co
Grand Rapids, Michigan 49516

 Inter-Varsity Press

BS
1151.52
.L66
2003

© 1991, 1995, 2003 by Tremper Longman III

Published by Baker Academic
a division of Baker Book House Company
P.O. Box 6287, Grand Rapids, MI 49516-6287
www.bakeracademic.com

and

Inter-Varsity Press
38 De Montfort Street
Leicester LE1 7GP
England
ivp@uccf.org.uk
www.ivpbooks.com

Printed in the United States of America

All rights reserved. No part of this publication may be reproduced, stored in a retrieval system, or transmitted in any form or by any means—for example, electronic, photocopy, recording—without the prior written permission of the publisher. The only exception is brief quotations in printed reviews.

Library of Congress Cataloging-in-Publication Data

Longman, Tremper.
    Old Testament commentary survey / Tremper Longman III.—3rd ed.
        p.   cm.
    Includes index.
    ISBN 0-8010-2629-6 (pbk.)
    1. Bible. O.T.—Commentaries—Bibliography. 2. Bible. O.T.—Commentaries—History and criticism. I. Title.
Z7772.A1L64 2003
[BS1151.52]
016.2217—dc21   2003052085

British Library Cataloguing in Publication Data

A catalogue record for this book is available from the British Library.

UK ISBN 0-85111-794-5

To
Alan Groves, Peter Enns, Doug Green, and Mike Kelly
Department of Old Testament, Westminster Theological
Seminary

Contents

Preface to the Third Edition

To be honest, I was for years ambivalent about updating the commentary guide. After all, it takes a tremendous amount of work. This explains, in part at least, why there has been a considerable time gap between the second (1995) and third editions. However, I receive an amazing number of e-mails from people who have found the guide useful as they consider what commentaries to buy. The selection is indeed quite staggering, especially for some biblical books. It is, therefore, helpful to get a preliminary, though brief, assessment of such matters as intended audience, emphases, theological and methodological perspective, and quality.

In the end, I am glad to have done the work necessary to produce this new edition. The work gave me the excuse to work more carefully with the commentaries that have appeared in the past seven years. What I saw was rather encouraging. The quality of most of the newer commentaries is quite good. During this time, new sets have appeared. If there is a trend, it is a healthy one: commentaries now take more seriously the need to bridge the ancient text to our modern situation. If there is one thing I would like to see in future commentaries, at least in those produced by the Christian community for the church, is more reflection on how the Old Testament message is appropriated by the New Testament.

Since there are so many new commentaries, I had to make many omissions. The largest change from the past is that this guide only concerns itself with commentaries, whereas earlier editions also covered other reference works. It is also impossible to be exhaustive in covering commentaries. There are omissions even here. I am mostly concerned with those commentaries that are widely sold. For one thing, this entails a concentration on sets rather than stand-alone commentaries. Even so, the choice of what is included in this volume and what is not is admittedly subjective.

Acknowledgments

When I began this project several years ago, I thought it would take a minimum amount of time and serve a limited readership. Many of my students had asked for my opinion on commentaries, but one of them, Eric Brauer, now a minister in Dublin, Ireland, kept pestering me to compile a list and to make it available in our seminary bookstore. I figured I could devote a few minutes each day to writing a brief review of the best commentaries I knew on certain biblical books. To make a long story short, Allan Fisher, director of publications at Baker Book House, caught wind of my efforts and asked me to expand the list to include yet more commentaries and also other reference books to serve as the Old Testament counterpart to Don Carson's *New Testament Commentary Survey* (5th ed., 2001). I did not realize how much work was involved; but now that it is over, I would like to express my appreciation to both Eric and Allan for their encouragement to write this guide. The second edition was produced under the editorship of Jim Weaver. Now that I have come to the third edition, I have a further friend to acknowledge and that is my present editor at Baker Book House, Jim Kinney.

Also, since the last edition, I have moved from Westminster Theological Seminary in Philadelphia to Westmont College in Santa Barbara, California. After eighteen wonderful years in Philadelphia, I would like to dedicate this book especially to my close friends and colleagues in the Old Testament department there: Alan Groves, Peter Enns, Doug Green, and Mike Kelly.

Abbreviations

AB	Anchor Bible
ANET	*Ancient Near Eastern Texts Relating to the Old Testament.* Edited by J. B. Pritchard. 3d ed. Princeton, 1969
BDB	Brown, F., S. R. Driver, and C. A. Briggs. *A Hebrew and English Lexicon of the Old Testament.* Oxford, 1907
BSC	Bible Student's Commentary
BST	Bible Speaks Today, The
CBC	Cambridge Bible Commentary
CC	Communicator's Commentary
DSB	Daily Study Bible, The
EBC	Expositor's Bible Commentary
FOTL	Forms of the Old Testament Literature
GKC	*Gesenius' Hebrew Grammar.* Edited by E. Kautzsch. Translated by A. E. Cowley. 2d ed. Oxford, 1910
IB	*Interpreter's Bible.* Edited by G. A. Buttrick et al. 12 vols. New York, 1951–1957
ICC	International Critical Commentary
Interp	Interpretation
ITC	International Theological Commentary

JPS	Jewish Publication Society
JSOT	*Journal for the Study of the Old Testament*
KB	Koehler, L., and W. Baumgartner, *Lexicon in Veteris Testamenti libros.* 2d ed. Leiden, 1958
NAC	New American Commentary
NCB	New Century Bible
NIB	New Interpreter's Bible
NIBCOT	New International Biblical Commentary on the Old Testament
NICOT	New International Commentary on the Old Testament
NIVAC	New International Version Application Commentary
OTL	Old Testament Library
OTM	Old Testament Message
OTS	Old Testament Studies
SHBC	Smyth and Helwys Bible Commentary
TBC	Torch Bible Commentaries
TDOT	*Theological Dictionary of the Old Testament.* Edited by G. J. Botterweck and H. Ringgren. Translated by J. T. Willis, G. W. Bromiley, and D. E. Green. 13 vols. Grand Rapids, 1974–
TOTC	Tyndale Old Testament Commentaries
WBC	Word Biblical Commentary
WEC	Wycliffe Exegetical Commentary

Introduction

Of making many books there is no end, and
much study wearies the body.

—Eccles. 12:12

While surveying the many commentaries listed in this guide, this verse came to mind more than once. Sometimes it seemed as if a new commentary appeared every week.

Upon more rational reflection, however, it is clear that there is a dearth of commentaries on the Old Testament. This situation is not simply because some commentaries are of little real worth, but also because there are only a few commentaries on the books of the Old Testament, although, at the time of the production of this third edition, this situation is changing. Furthermore, no single commentary, no matter how exhaustive, can provide all the information the reader might want and need. In addition, commentaries are addressed to specialized audiences. A commentary written with the needs of the layperson in mind will often not be of real interest to the scholar, while one written for a scholarly audience is often of no use to the layperson. Ministers have enough training to be interested in answers to technical questions, but also want help in making the text relevant to the people in their congregation.

Who Should Read This Guide?

There are many commentaries available. As a specialist in Old Testament, I do not think I have been asked any question more frequently than "What's the best commentary on . . . ?"

This guide is for anyone, layperson or minister, who desires to buy a commentary. It lists a number of works available for each book of the Old Testament, briefly summarizes their emphases and viewpoints, and evaluates them. This guide will be helpful to seminary students beginning to build the reference library that will be crucial to their preaching and teaching ministries.

Evaluation

Some might disagree with me in the value I assign to individual commentaries. It is accordingly of some interest to know what I value in a commentary and the perspective from which I write.

I represent an evangelical approach to the Old Testament and, accordingly, give high marks to good commentaries that come from a similar perspective. However, it is important to emphasize the adjective "good." I am particularly hard on shallow or incompetent commentaries that come from the perspective I advocate. Similarly, I can appreciate and learn from writers who write from a perspective different than my own.

I evaluate commentaries on a 1-to-5 scale. One or two asterisks indicate that the commentary is inferior or deficient, and I discourage its purchase. Four or five asterisks is a high mark. Three, obviously, means a commentary is good but not great.

I also indicate who would most benefit from the commentary under consideration. There are three categories: L(ayperson); M(inister) (seminary students should consider themselves in this category); and S(cholar). I provide page counts for each volume, with small roman numerals indicating the pages of introductory material.

For a similar guide to the New Testament, please consult D. A. Carson, *New Testament Commentary Survey* (5th ed., Baker/Inter-Varsity, 2001).

The Use and Abuse of Commentaries

There is a right way and a wrong way to use a commentary. Actually, there are two wrong ways. The first is to ignore completely the use of commentaries. Some people do not consult commentaries because they believe that, since all Christians are equal as they approach the Scriptures, scholars have no privileged insight into the biblical text. The second error is to become overly dependent on commentaries. "These people have devoted their whole lives to the study of the Bible. How can my opinion measure up to theirs?"

Those holding the first position are wrong because they forget that God gives different gifts to different people in the church. Not all people are equally adept at understanding the Bible and teaching it to others (1 Cor. 12:12–31). Those holding the second position err in the opposite direction. They forget that God has given believers the Spirit by which they can discern spiritual things (1 Cor. 2:14–16).

The right way to use a commentary is as a help. We should first of all study a passage without reference to any helps. Only after coming to an initial understanding of the passage should we consult commentaries.

Neither should we let commentaries bully us. Many times they will be of great help, but sometimes the reader will be right and the commentaries will be wrong.

One-Volume Commentaries

One-volume commentaries are commentaries on the whole Bible bound in one volume. They generally have between 1,000 and 1,500 pages. While commentaries on individual books are too short to provide insight into a text, such volumes are handy to have around for a quick orientation to a book or passage of Scripture. They are relatively inexpensive and are good choices for laypeople who do not want to invest in a series. There are also some excellent study Bibles available that basically function as one-volume commentaries. The best out there right now is the *NIV Study Bible*.

Carson, D. A., R. T. France, J. A. Motyer, and G. J. Wenham, eds. *New Bible Commentary: Twenty-first Century Edition.* Inter-Varsity, 1994. 1,455 pp.

This volume is a thorough revision of the earlier *New Bible Commentary Revised*. It brings the latter up to date through the work of many leading Old and New Testament scholars. The introductory and general articles are helpful and well-written. LM*****

Elwell, W. A., ed. *Baker Commentary on the Bible*. Baker, 1989. 1,230 pp.

This volume is written from an evangelical perspective. It provides a good, concise theological and historical analysis of all the books of the Bible. Contributors include Raymond Dillard, Royce Gruenler, Victor Hamilton, R. K. Harrison, James Hoffmeier, Elmer Martens, Douglas Moo, Stephen Noll, R. D. Patterson, Willem Van Gemeren, and Herbert Wolf. LM****

Guthrie, D., and J. A. Motyer, eds. *The Eerdmans Bible Commentary.* Eerdmans, 1970. 1,310 pp.

This volume is excellent, although it is now getting a little dated. (It used to be known as *The New Bible Commentary.*) Its many contributors are consistently good. The theological perspective is conservative. It is exegetically insightful and sound. Some of the notable contributions are by M. Kline (Genesis), O. T. Allis (Leviticus), A. Millard (Jeremiah), D. Kidner (Isaiah), J. Baldwin (Ruth and Esther), D. J. Wiseman (Haggai), and R. K. Harrison (Deuteronomy). LM***

Pfeiffer, C. F., and E. F. Harrison. *The Wycliffe Bible Commentary.* Moody, 1962. xv/1,525 pp.

This is a fine one-volume commentary. Its contributors span the evangelical spectrum. Note the articles by M. Kline (Deuteronomy and Job), E. Smick (Numbers), and S. Woudstra (Song of Solomon). LM**

Walton, J. H., V. H. Matthews, and M. W. Chavalas. *The IVP Bible Background Commentary: Old Testament.* Inter-Varsity, 2000. 832 pp.

This easy-to-use reference book concentrates on the ancient Near Eastern background that otherwise is so difficult for the modern lay reader, but that is also incredibly illuminating. LM*****

Commentary Sets

Publishers have found that commentaries sell best in a set. There are a number of commentary sets currently in production. The following list serves two purposes. It will describe more fully and evaluate those sets that are written by one or two authors. Second, it will describe the method of other sets by multiple authors. The individual volumes found in this second group are described and evaluated in the following section, which proceeds book by book through the Bible. It should be noted that sets with a number of different authors often vary in quality. It is often best to choose among commentaries rather than committing oneself to a single set of commentaries. The asterisks indicate those series whose individual volumes I try to include consistently.

*Anchor Bible (AB). Ed. D. N. Freedman. Doubleday.

The Anchor Bible is an indispensable tool for scholars and certain ministers, but often fails in its attempt to communicate with laypersons. It usually emphasizes philology, historical background, and text, rather than theology. The volumes range in quality from excellent to horrible. MS***

Berit Olam. Ed. D. W. Cotter. Michael Glazier.

This series is just underway and provides a focus on the literary analysis of the books. This means different things to the contributors, as may be seen by comparing J. T.

Walsh's close reading of 1 Kings with D. Jobling's post-modern analysis of 1 Samuel. MS***

*Bible Speaks Today, The (BST). Ed. Alec Motyer (Old Testament), John Stott (New Testament), and Derek Tidball (the new BST Bible Themes). Inter-Varsity.

The purpose of this set is to write on the biblical text in a way that engages the reader. In other words, its volumes can be read cover to cover; they are not simply reference tools. The series is readable, accurate, and relevant. LM****

Calvin's Commentaries. 22 vols. Reprint, Baker.

These commentaries find their origin in Calvin's sermons, but they are learned and theologically insightful. It is no wonder that Calvin is called the "prince of expositors." Calvin does comment on language occasionally, but one will have to consult a more recent commentary because of discoveries in the Hebrew language. He does not cover the whole Old Testament. Volumes are missing between Judges and Job. The five-volume commentary on Psalms is wonderful. Unfortunately, Calvin harmonizes Exodus to Deuteronomy. LMS*****

Cambridge Bible Commentary (CBC). Ed. P. R. Ackroyd, A. R. C. Leaney, and J. W. Packer. Cambridge University Press.

This series is composed of short and readable commentaries on all the books of the Old Testament and the Apocrypha. They intend to bring the fruits of contemporary scholarship to educated laypersons. The volumes also intend to explicate the New English Bible, which is the base of the commentary. They concentrate on both historical and theological issues. A selection of volumes includes R. E. Clements on Exodus; P. R. Ackroyd on Samuel; R. J. Coggins on Chronicles; J. D. W. Watts on the Minor Prophets; and R. N. Whybray on Proverbs. LM***

Communicator's Commentary (CC). 23 vols. Ed. Lloyd Ogilvie. Word. (Now available as Mastering the Old Testament.)

This energetic series is directed toward pastors and other Christian leaders who teach. For the most part, the volumes meet their intended goal and are backed by solid scholarship. The volumes are also very readable. LM***

Daily Study Bible (DSB). 24 vols. Ed. J. C. L. Gibson. Westminster John Knox.

The DSB is the Old Testament counterpart to Barclay's New Testament commentaries. The name derives from the fact that the commentators have divided the text (RSV) into portions that can be read in a single day's devotional. The commentary is directed toward the layperson and encourages an expositional and theological reading of the text. LM****

Expositor's Bible Commentary (EBC). Ed. F. E. Gaebelein. Zondervan.

This is a multivolume set, but each volume contains comments on a number of biblical books and is authored by different scholars. The authors come from a general evangelical background and articulate a predominantly premillennial perspective. The series is geared for preachers, teachers, and students. There are six volumes on the Old Testament. The scholars are for the most part quite capable in historical-grammatical exegesis. LM***

*Forms of the Old Testament Literature (FOTL). Ed. R. Knierim and G. M. Tucker. Eerdmans.

When completed, this series will have twenty-four volumes. The title of the series indicates its focus on a form-critical approach to the text. Judged in the light of their purpose, these are excellent commentaries. Scholars will find these books invaluable. S****

*Hermeneia. Ed. F. C. Cross et al. Fortress/SCM.

A number of the volumes in this series are translations of original German works, although there are some English contributions. The quality of the series is high. It intends to deliver the best of historical and critical scholarship, and usually succeeds. There are some classic works in this series. S*****

International Critical Commentary (ICC). T & T Clark.

These are highly technical studies of philology and text. They are best used by specialists and retain their value in spite of their age. A new series is presently being written. S***

International Theological Commentary (ITC). Handsel.

This is a series of short commentaries written from a third-world perspective. The purpose is both to shake off some of the assumptions of Western readers and to connect the text with contemporary issues. It often provides interesting insight into the Bible. At other times, however, these volumes are scarcely distinguishable from traditional commentaries. LM**

*Interpretation (Interp). Ed. J. L. Mays. John Knox.

This series bridges the gap between scholarly investigation and contemporary relevance. Moderately critical, the series is readable and interesting. LM****

*JPS Torah Commentary. Ed. N. Sarna. Jewish Publication Society.

The series, as the title indicates, will cover only the first five books of the Hebrew Bible. The commentary prints the Hebrew text and gives copious comments on philology, history of research (with very interesting comments from rabbinic material), and theology. The content and the production of the volumes are first-rate. MS*****

Keil-Delitzsch. 10 vols. Eerdmans.

C. F. Keil and F. Delitzsch were orthodox Lutheran Old Testament scholars from Germany in the latter half of the nineteenth century. Their expositions, although dated, are solid and competent. They often give helpful theological commentary as well. This set is fairly inexpensive and makes a good backbone to a minister's library. LM****

Knox Preaching Guides. Ed. J. H. Hayes. John Knox.

These short paperbacks offer assistance to ministers as they prepare to preach. A number of notable contributors, including W. Brueggemann, J. J. Collins, W. Roth, E. Achtemeier, and J. G. Gammie. Moderately critical for the most part. M***

Layman's Bible Commentary. Westminster/John Knox.

Short, concise commentaries written for the layperson by critical scholars of the past generation. LM**

Leupold's Commentaries. Baker.

Leupold was a conservative Lutheran who wrote on many Old Testament books (Genesis, Psalms, Ecclesiastes, Isaiah, Daniel, and Zechariah). Leupold's work has value, but he tends to write more like a systematic theologian than a biblical exegete. LM**

Minor Prophets, The. Ed. T. McComiskey. Baker.

In most series, the Minor Prophets are given short shrift. This series intends to give the Minor Prophets their due. While not every contribution is the best on its particular book, this is the best anthology of commentaries on the Minor Prophets available. MS*****

*New American Commentary (NAC). Ed. E. Ray Clendenen. Broadman.

This relatively new series is making a strong entry into the field of commentaries. Based on the NIV text, it is an expository commentary with an emphasis on the theological message of the Bible as a whole. It adopts a clear evangelical approach to the text. The first few volumes that have appeared are for the most part highly competent, but not outstanding. MS***

*New Century Bible (NCB). OT ed., R. E. Clements. Sheffield.

The New Century Bible is a predominantly British project based on the Revised Standard Version. Many of the volumes seem restricted by the format. As a series, it is weak. There are, however, some very fine volumes. The volumes range from moderately critical to heavily critical. LM* *

*New International Biblical Commentary on the Old Testament (NIBCOT) Ed. R. L. Hubbard, Jr., and R. Johnston. Hendrickson/Paternoster.

This series is committed to what the editors call "believing criticism," which tries to navigate between a kind of criticism that never gets to the meaning of the final form of the text and a theological dogmatism. LM* * * *

*New International Commentary on the Old Testament (NICOT). Ed. R. L. Hubbard Jr. Eerdmans.

This series was originally begun in the 1950s under E. J. Young's editorship, but was stalled after the editor produced his three-volume Isaiah commentary. Young's commentary has since been removed. The series is evangelical and scholarly, but written in a way that laypeople can understand. Technical issues as well as theological commentary are found in these commentaries. R. Hubbard has taken over since the death of R. K. Harrison. MS* * * *

*New International Version Application Commentary (NIVAC). Ed. A. Dearman, R. Hubbard, T. Longman, and John Walton. Zondervan/Hodder & Stoughton.

NIVAC comments on each unit under three topics: original meaning, bridging contexts, and contemporary significance. Excellent for the preacher. LM* * * * *

New Interpreter's Bible (NIB). Ed. L. E. Keck et al. Abingdon.

This series replaces the long-honored, original *Interpreter's Bible* that was produced in the 1950s. The format is a cross between a set and individual book commentaries. The Old Testament is covered in six volumes. The commentary has two sections: a more technical exegetical section and an expository section. A diversity of theological viewpoints is represented, but whether evangelical or not, all the contributors seem committed to the theological authority of the text. LM**

*Old Testament Library (OTL). Ed. P. Ackroyd et al. Westminster/SCM.

This is a distinguished collection of commentaries written in the critical tradition. Many, but not all, are translations of earlier German works. OTL includes, besides the commentaries, Eichrodt's *Theology*, Beyerlin's study of related ancient Near Eastern texts, and Soggin's history. MS***

Old Testament Message (OTM). Ed. C. Stuhlmueller and M. McNamara. Michael Glazier.

OTM is planned to be a twenty-three-volume set, geared for laypeople. While each volume is written by a Catholic scholar, it is hoped that the appeal will be much broader. The method is moderately critical with a premium on clarity, theology, and relevance. LM***

Torch Bible Commentaries (TBC). Ed. J. Marsh, A. Richardson, and R. Gregor Smith. SCM.

This series is very similar in intent, scope, and approach to the Cambridge Bible Commentaries. The contributors were asked to make the results of modern scholarship accessible to educated laypeople within the church. Two notable contributions include J. H. Eaton on Psalms and C. R. North on Isaiah 40–55. The commentary is based on the Authorized Version. LM***

*Tyndale Old Testament Commentaries (TOTC). Ed. D. J. Wiseman. Inter-Varsity.

These commentaries are authored by respected English, South African, Australian, Irish, and American evangelical scholars. They are in the main directed toward a nonspecialist audience. They emphasize exegesis. They are brief, but usually informative. LM****

*Word Biblical Commentary (WBC). Ed. J. D. W. Watts (OT). Nelson/Paternoster.

These commentaries are written by evangelicals identified in the preface as those committed "to Scripture as divine revelation, and to the truth and power of the Christian gospel." This definition allows for the wide-ranging approaches to the Bible found in the series. Not everyone will be satisfied that a given commentary is evangelical in its theological orientation, although most of the volumes clearly are. These commentaries are very learned, and provide their own translation with philological, textual, and literary notes. Theological message is also treated, but, with a few exceptions, these theological comments rarely bridge the gap to the New Testament. MS****

Individual Commentaries

Genesis

Aalders, G. C. *Genesis.* 2 vols. BSC. Zondervan, 1981. 311 pp. and 228 pp.

This is an English translation of a commentary originally published in Dutch in 1949. Although somewhat dated, Aalders's work retains its value as a theological commentary. Writing from within the Reformed tradition, Aalders shows great exegetical skill and theological insight. MS***

Atkinson, D. *The Message of Genesis 1–11: The Dawn of Creation.* BST. Inter-Varsity, 1990. 190 pp.

A brief, expository, and devotional reading of the first part of the Book of Genesis. Atkinson is insightful and knowledgeable. LM***

Baldwin, J. G. *The Message of Genesis 12–50: From Abraham to Joseph.* BST. Inter-Varsity, 1986. 224 pp.

Baldwin writes in a popular style, yet there is no doubt that considerable scholarly research stands behind her commentary. Her approach to Genesis 12–50 is traditional, yet not stodgy. LM***

Boice, J. M. *Genesis.* 2d ed. 3 vols. Baker, 1998. 1,303 pp.

Boice, a popular Presbyterian preacher, expectedly puts a heavy emphasis on the application of the text. Unfortunately, his treatment of Old Testament narrative tends

to be highly moralistic in ways that the text does not intend. LM**

Briscoe, S. *Genesis.* CC. Word, 1987. 414 pp.

Briscoe does a good job navigating the difficult interpretive issues of Genesis. Not that he is always right, but he
exercises fairly sensible judgment. The volume, in keeping with the purpose of the commentary, is sermonic
and anecdotal, not exegetical or biblical-theological.
However, what it does, it does well. LM***

Brueggemann, W. *Genesis.* Interp. Westminster John Knox,
1982. viii/384 pp.

Brueggemann, although a moderately critical scholar, is
always stimulating and insightful. His commentary concentrates on the final form of the text and focuses prin-
cipally on the theology of the book. LM****

Cassuto, U. *From Adam to Abraham: A Commentary on
the Book of Genesis.* Trans. I. Abrahams. 2 vols. Magnes,
1964. xviii/323 pp. and xiv/386 pp.

This is an excellent commentary on the first eleven
chapters of Genesis. Cassuto, a conservative Jewish writer,
died unexpectedly before the book was completed. He is
a brilliant philologist and literary scholar. He, interestingly, goes against the scholarly tide and rejects the Documentary Hypothesis. S***

Coats, G. W. *Genesis with an Introduction to Narrative
Literature.* FOTL. Eerdmans, 1983. xiii/322 pp.

Definitely one of the best volumes in the series thus far,
this commentary nonetheless is difficult to wade through
due to its focus on form-critical issues. Coats is most
helpful when he deals with narrative issues from a literary standpoint. He is least helpful when he spends time
analyzing the sources of the narrative rather than con-
centrating on the final form of the text. S***

Davidson, R. *Genesis 1–11.* CBC. Cambridge University
Press, 1973. x/118 pp.

This brief commentary presents a critical perspective on the first chapters of Genesis to an educated, popular audience. The introduction presents a source-critical approach to the question of composition and deals with myth and the stories of Genesis. LM**

Gibson, J. C. L. *Genesis.* DSB. 2 vols. Westminster John Knox, 1981. ix/214 pp. and 322 pp.

In keeping with the nature of the series, Gibson writes in a popular vein. He helpfully opens up the text for lay understanding, showing the relevance of Genesis for the Christian. He is less helpful when he describes the composition of the book along the lines of older source criticism. LM***

Gowan, D. E. *Genesis 1–11.* ITC. Handsel, 1988. ix/125 pp.

A short theological study of the first eleven chapters of the Bible. While there is considerable theological reflection, the book also displays a fair share of typical critical assumptions. Gowan's treatment of the relationship between the theology and history of Genesis is quite superficial and will not satisfy many. While many of the commentaries in this series come from a third-world perspective, this one does not. It also fails to interact with contemporary social and political issues to the extent of many of the other volumes. LM**

Hamilton, V. P. *The Book of Genesis.* 2 vols. NICOT. Eerdmans, 1990, 1995. 522 pp. and 774 pp.

Hamilton does an excellent job interpreting the text in a positive way as well as handling the difficult questions of the book (creation story, history of patriarchs, religion of patriarchs). Between Wenham and Hamilton, Genesis is well covered. MS*****

Hartley, J. E. *Genesis.* NIBCOT. Hendrickson/Paternoster, 2000. xvii/393 pp.

I cannot always agree with Hartley's analysis of the structure of the Book of Genesis or with his analysis of sections of it as a palistrophe (the arrangement of material in a V-shaped pattern, also known as chiasm), but Hartley nonetheless offers a clear and straightforward analysis of the Book of Genesis. The depth of exposition is constrained by the series. His arguments in favor of Mosaic involvement in the production of the book and also in favor of the patriarchal narratives is refreshing. LM****

Herbert, A. S. *Genesis 12–50.* TBC. SCM, 1962. 160 pp.

Herbert assumes the literary introduction of Richardson. He believes that the patriarchal period began in 1650 B.C., a view not widely held today by liberal or conservative scholars. He sees the uniqueness of Israelite religion not in monotheism but in divine-human personal relationships. LM**

Kidner, D. *Genesis.* TOTC. Inter-Varsity, 1967. 224 pp.

This is an excellent commentary within the parameters of the series. Since it is so brief, it cannot hope to fully comment on the text. It is noticeably lacking (by design) substantial philological notes. It is written from a solidly conservative standpoint. This is a good starter commentary for the layperson. LM***

Maher, M. *Genesis.* OTM. Michael Glazier, 1982. 279 pp.

The volume may have some value in its theological commentary. It presents the rather naive critical view that Genesis is a "statement of religious truths" rather than history. Maher accepts the now dated Documentary Hypothesis, although he notes challenges to it in passing. LM**

Mathews, K. A. *Genesis 1–11:26.* NAC. Broadman, 1996. 526 pp.

Mathews has produced an excellent study of the primeval history with an emphasis on the text as literature and theology. He does not shrink from the difficult historical and philological issues either. He navigates well the relationship between these chapters and ancient

Near Eastern literature. He intends to complete his study of Genesis in the future. LM★★★★

Richardson, A. *Genesis 1–11.* TBC. SCM, 1953. 134 pp.

Richardson gives a brief exposition of source criticism, although aware that the traditional sources contain older material. He treats the main stories of the first few chapters of Genesis as parables, avoiding the label "myth" because the lay mind equates that term with falsity. LM★★

Ross, Allen P. *Creation and Blessing: A Guide to the Study and Exposition of Genesis.* Baker, 1988. 744 pp.

The book opens with a short introduction to the whole book, stating the author's method of approach to Genesis. Ross presents an evangelical alternative to the documentary approach. The bulk of his treatment, however, is more like a running exposition with an emphasis on theology. As such it is often insightful and helpful. A good book, especially for pastors preaching through the Book of Genesis. LM★★★★

Sarna, N. M. *Understanding Genesis: The Heritage of Biblical Israel.* Schocken, 1966. 245 pp.

This readable commentary is written from a pious Jewish perspective that takes into account a moderate historical-critical approach and attempts to make Genesis meaningful and relevant to an educated lay audience. Sarna believes that God can work through four sources (JEDP) as well as a unified book and further argues that historical criticism supports rather than denies faith. Short, but readable, with an emphasis on interpretation and comparative studies. MS★★★

Sarna, N. M. *Genesis.* JPS Torah Commentary. Jewish Publication Society, 1989. xxi/414 pp.

This commentary is considerably more academic in approach than the one published in 1966. It studies the text in a verse-by-verse, virtually word-by-word manner.

Although Sarna recognizes the composite nature of Genesis, he treats the book as a whole in the commentary. His emphasis, although he deals with other aspects of the text, is on Near Eastern background and Jewish tradition. MS****

Scullion, J. J. *Genesis: A Commentary for Students, Teachers, and Preachers.* OTS. Liturgical/Michael Glazier, 1992. xviii/366 pp.

This commentary, published right after Scullion's death, is a strong, traditionally critical approach to the book. Not that the author lacks his own distinctive approach, but he fails to take into account important recent developments in literary approaches and also recent insights from source criticism. Nonetheless, he is strong on the history of research up to the most recent developments and also on ancient Near Eastern background. M***

Skinner, J. *A Critical and Exegetical Commentary on Genesis.* ICC. T & T Clark, 1910. lxvi/552 pp.

This volume represents the best of turn-of-the-century critical thought. Skinner does a detailed source analysis of the book along the lines of the Documentary Hypothesis. This is an extremely detailed commentary. Helpful grammatical information may be found here. The book is in small print, however, and is often hard to read. Not recommended for the layperson or pastor. S**

Speiser, E. A. *Genesis.* AB. Doubleday, 1964. lxxiv/379 pp.

Speiser takes a fairly classical, critical approach to the Book of Genesis in the delineation of sources. The introduction separates P, J, and E sources (the order in which they appear in the book) and then discusses the residue. Speiser is of some help in matters of language, since he was one of the preeminent Semitic linguists of his day. This commentary is a must-buy for the scholar, but probably of little use to anyone else. S**

von Rad, G. *Genesis.* OTL. Westminster/SCM, 1972. 440 pp.

An insightful, but critical, commentary on Genesis. Von Rad is sensitive to theology and literature. He is not known for his work on the Hebrew language. He argues for the Hexateuch and delineates sources. S***

Waltke, B. K., and Cathi J. Fredricks. *Genesis*. Zondervan, 2001. 656 pp.

This commentary is not in a series but is well worth tracking down and adding to a reference library. Waltke is the dean of evangelical biblical studies, and this commentary is exegetically insightful and theologically rich. LM*****

Walton, J. H. *Genesis*. NIVAC. Zondervan/Hodder & Stoughton, 2001. 752 pp.

Walton's commentary is stimulating and well-written. He navigates the difficult issues of the book well. Unfortunately, he rarely comments on the relationship between Genesis and the New Testament. LM****

Wenham, G. J. *Genesis 1–15*. WBC. Nelson/Paternoster, 1987. *Genesis 16–50*. WBC. Nelson/Paternoster, 1994. liii/353 pp. and 555 pp.

Wenham is one of the finest evangelical commentators today. His commentary on Genesis shows his high level of scholarship and his exegetical sensitivity. He represents a conservative approach to Genesis, but does not completely reject source theory. LM*****

Westermann, C. *Genesis*. 3 vols. Continental Commentary. Fortress/SPCK, 1984–86. xii/636 pp., 604 pp., 269 pp.

These three volumes were originally published in German between 1974 and 1982. This commentary is a fully conceived approach that takes into account text, form, setting, interpretation, purpose, and thrust. It also provides excellent bibliographies for each section and synthesizes previous research. It claims to be the first major commentary on Genesis in decades, and is from a moderately critical stance. MS****

Youngblood, R. *The Book of Genesis: An Introductory Commentary.* Baker, 1991. 295 pp.

This volume is a reworking of two volumes that Youngblood published in 1976 and 1980. The focus is on the book's teaching, not on philology or form. The introduction, which deals with questions of authorship and date, among other issues, is adequate for the volume, which is directed toward laypeople. The writing style is engaging and clear. LM***

Exodus

Burns, R. J. *Exodus, Leviticus, Numbers.* OTM. Michael Glazier, 1983. 298 pp.

The author takes a traditional literary-critical approach to these three pentateuchal books. She asserts that Exodus "must be read as a religious creed and not as a historical chronicle" (19). She does not treat every chapter of all three books, and Leviticus and Numbers get less attention than Exodus. LM**

Cassuto, U. *Commentary on the Book of Exodus.* Trans. I. Abrahams. Magnes, 1967. xvi/509 pp.

Cassuto rejects the Documentary Hypothesis and explains the existing text. He is sensitive to the literary artistry of Exodus and brilliant in his philological analysis. See also comments under his commentary on Genesis. S***

Childs, B. S. *The Book of Exodus.* OTL. Westminster/SCM, 1974. xxv/659 pp.

This is one of the best commentaries on Exodus. Childs divides his commentary into different sections, including textual criticism and philology, critical methods, Old Testament context, New Testament context, and history of interpretation. Although representing a critical perspective, this volume is valuable to evangelical ministers. MS*****

Coats, G. W. *Exodus 1–18*. FOTL. Eerdmans, 1999. xiv/178 pp.

The preface explains the difficult journey that this volume had to reach publication and this in large part explains why this book is not even close to being up to the standard of the rest of the series. S**

Cole, R. Alan. *Exodus*. TOTC. Inter-Varsity, 1973. 239 pp.

As is the case with all the volumes in this series, this is a book with all the inherent disadvantages of a short commentary. There is not much of general introduction or interaction with source criticism, but there is an excellent theological introduction. It is definitely worth the price. LM***

Dunnam, M. D. *Exodus*. CC. Word, 1987. 395 pp.

As with most of the volumes in this series, this one is heavier on anecdotes and sermonic application than a serious study of the book's content. Of course, such a study can be a useful supplement to other commentaries, especially for ministers as they seek to bridge the gap between the ancient world and that of a modern congregation. LM***

Durham, J. I. *Exodus*. WBC. Nelson/Paternoster, 1987. xxxiv/516 pp.

The strength of this commentary is its focus on the theology of the text. Its weakness is its casual attitude toward the historicity of Exodus. Durham identifies the heart of the book's message as the presence of God with God's people. MS****

Ellison, H. L. *Exodus*. DSB. Westminster, 1982. 203 pp.

Ellison does a good job explaining the text to the modern lay reader. He is insightful, but the commentary is too brief. The introduction is short even for the series, and makes only passing reference to the critical problems of history. Ellison emphasizes theology and is committed to a New Testament approach after studying the text in its Old Testament context. LM**

Enns, P. *Exodus.* NIVAC. Zondervan/Hodder & Stoughton, 2000. 448 pp.

Enns has produced an incredibly insightful theological study of the book. He also deals well with the important historical issues, but not from a technical standpoint. This commentary is ideal for those preaching on Exodus, because he so thoughtfully explores the book's trajectory toward the New Testament gospel. LM*****

Fretheim, T. E. *Exodus.* Interp. Westminster John Knox, 1990. xii/321 pp.

This very readable volume is stimulating in discussing the theological message of the Book of Exodus. Fretheim might be described as a moderate critic who concentrates on the final form of the text. This volume is not particularly helpful on the more technical aspects of the book. LM****

Gispen, W. H. *Exodus.* BSC. Zondervan, 1982. 335 pp.

Gispen's work was originally published in Dutch in 1951. It is full of helpful exegetical and theological insights from a Reformed perspective. MS***

Hyatt, J. B. *Exodus.* NCB. Sheffield, 1971. 351 pp.

Hyatt takes a critical approach to the Book of Exodus. His comments are brief and sketchy. There is very little theological or literary exposition. The book, however, has a series of excurses on various topics of interest, such as the origin of Mosaic Yahwism and the Passover. Worthwhile only if one is interested in a critical perspective on an issue. S**

Noth, M. *Exodus.* Trans. J. Bowden. OTL. Westminster/ SCM, 1962. 283 pp.

Noth is one of the most important German critical scholars of this century. He concentrates on historical and literary issues from a critical perspective. This is an important piece of scholarship, but will not help the pastor or layperson. S****

Propp, W. H. C. *Exodus 1–18.* AB. Doubleday, 1998. xl/680 pp.

Propp's commentary has some unique features compared to other volumes in the series. For one thing, each section begins with comments on text, source, and redaction criticism. Also, contrary to the practice of most biblical scholars, Propp marks a speculative remark as speculation (other scholars will judge that some of his unmarked comments are equally speculative!). His opening translation is quite literal, even awkwardly so. Many readers will find these features a bit confusing and off-putting, but there are some excellent insights into the text. MS****

Sarna, N. M. *Exodus.* JPS Torah Commentary. Jewish Publication Society, 1991. 304 pp.

Sarna is one of the masters of commentary-writing on the Torah. This volume is noticeably shorter than the others in the series and lacks their vitality. Nonetheless, the serious student should consult it. MS***

Leviticus

Bellinger, W. H., Jr. *Leviticus, Numbers.* NIBCOT. Hendrickson/Paternoster, 2001. 338 pp.

This is a fine commentary that provides an interesting and significant reading of the Books of Leviticus and Numbers. The series does not allow Bellinger to display it very often, but serious research lies behind his accessible prose. Bellinger does not ignore New Testament connections, but this part could have been strengthened. LM****

Demarest, G. W. *Leviticus.* CC. Word, 1990. 286 pp.

Demarest confesses that he struggled to come to grips with the meaning and significance of this biblical book. The results are often satisfying, and he provides a helpful introduction to the relevance of Leviticus, especially geared to those teaching or preaching from it. The commentary should be supplemented by a more academic volume for serious study. LM***

Gerstenberger, E. *Leviticus*. OTL. Westminster John Knox, 1996. 456 pp.

Situates the material late, to the fifth century B.C. Writes very clearly on a level that even laypeople will be able to understand, though some of the technical discussions will not be of interest to them. This is a good, solid commentary from a critical perspective, but other commentaries on the book are better. MS***

Harrison, R. K. *Leviticus*. TOTC. Inter-Varsity, 1980. 252 pp.

Harrison is one of the most competent Old Testament evangelical scholars today. The commentary is too short to compete with Wenham's volume, but still well worth having. LM***

Hartley, J. E. *Leviticus*. WBC. Nelson/Paternoster, 1992. lxxiii/496 pp.

This commentary is substantial in quality as well as quantity. Hartley approaches his task with the tools of the philologist, literary scholar, and theologian. The approach to authorship is extremely helpful. There is also a lengthy introductory essay on the history of interpretation of the book. MS*****

Knight, G. A. F. *Leviticus*. DSB. Westminster, 1981. 173 pp.

While moderately critical in his approach to Leviticus, Knight provides a helpful exposition of what the book means in its Old Testament context and devotes considerable attention to its relevance for the Christian. One of the better volumes of the series. LM****

Levine, B. A. *Leviticus*. JPS Torah Commentary. Jewish Publication Society, 1989. xlvi/284 pp.

Levine writes with the educated layperson in mind. His

writing style is accessible, while he treats topics that the scholar would be interested in. Levine is one of the true experts on Leviticus and presents a stimulating and important study of the book within its context in the ancient world. He is also theologically sensitive. MS****

Milgrom, J. *Leviticus 1–16.* AB. Doubleday, 1991. *Leviticus 17–22.* AB. Doubleday, 2000. *Leviticus 23–27.* AB. Doubleday, 2001. xviii/1,163 pp., xvii/624 pp., and xxi/818 pp.

Milgrom divides Leviticus into three parts. This first volume of his commentary covers the section owing its origin to P; the second volume covers the section that he argues comes from H (the Holiness Code). However, he is most concerned with the final form of the text, not its prehistory. Milgrom is clearly the world's leading expert on Leviticus. He writes from a moderately critical point of view, informed by his wealth of knowledge of early Jewish interpretation. MS*****

Noordtzij, A. *Leviticus.* BSC. Zondervan, 1982. xi/280 pp.

This commentary is a translation of a Dutch original and presents a basic evangelical approach to the text, although Noordtzij believes that some of the laws are post-Mosaic. He is theologically sensitive and responsible. MS***

Porter, J. R. *Leviticus.* CBC. Cambridge University Press, 1976. x/232 pp.

This is a brief but well-written study of a difficult biblical book. Porter presents a clearly critical position on Leviticus. He shows sensitivity to theological issues and to the relevance of the book for today. LM***

Rooker, M. F. *Leviticus.* NAC. Broadman & Holman, 2000. 352 pp.

Rooker writes in an engaging style and has an eye on making the book relevant for the Christian reader by pointing out connections to New Testament theology. LM****

Snaith, N. H. *Leviticus and Numbers.* NCB. Reprint, Sheffield, 1977. xii/352 pp.

Snaith is a competent Hebraist, so it is not surprising
that the strength of this volume is in textual criticism
and philology. The commentary suffers from the re-
straints of the series. It is really a brief, sketchy commentary on the RSV. Although there is little theological
reflection, the text is clearly written from a critical perspective. S**

Wenham, G. J. *The Book of Leviticus.* NICOT. Eerdmans,
1979. xiii/362 pp.

Wenham has provided a fascinating and extremely helpful discussion of what most Christians regard as a drab
book. He does an excellent job in explaining the holiness
laws and their function in ancient Israel. It is a well-
written commentary. MS*****

Numbers

Ashley, T. R. *The Book of Numbers.* NICOT. Eerdmans,
1993. xvi/667 pp.

While Wenham's short commentary is excellent, the
NICOT format allows Ashley to delve more deeply and
widely into the issues surrounding this important,
though neglected, book of the Pentateuch. Ashley writes
in a very readable style. He not only deals with the technical problems of the book, but also demonstrates the
relevance of the book for theology. He interacts with
previous scholarship, but not obsessively. MS****

Bellinger, W. H., Jr. *Leviticus, Numbers.* NIBCOT. Hen-
drickson/Paternoster, 2001. 338 pp.

See under Leviticus.

Brown, R. *The Message of Numbers.* BST. Inter-Varsity,
2002. 288 pp.

A readable and informed study of this often-neglected
book. In keeping with the series, Brown emphasizes the

theological meaning and the contemporary significance of the book. LM***

Budd, P. J. *Numbers.* WBC. Nelson/Paternoster, 1984. xxxii/ 409 pp.

This is a well-researched and thought-out commentary. It employs a source-critical methodology in a way that will offend some evangelicals. It is weak in biblical theology. S**

Cole, R. D. *Numbers.* NAC. Broadman, 2001. 590 pp.

A substantial, well-written commentary that navigates the scholarly literature well, incorporating what is good and rejecting what is bad, while still keeping its individual contribution. Cole gives an excellent argument in favor of an essential or core Mosaic authorship of Numbers. The book's real strength is in its sensitive theological reading. LM*****

Gray, G. B. *Numbers.* ICC. T & T Clark, 1903. lii/489 pp.

This commentary is highly technical, very critical, and somewhat dated. Its valuable points have been incorporated into other, more recent commentaries. S**

Harrison, R. K. *Numbers.* WEC. Moody, 1990. xvi/452 pp.

This is the first Old Testament volume to appear in Moody's new series. This particular volume takes a verse-by-verse approach (as opposed to Silva's Philippians commentary in the same series). It emphasizes exegesis and exposition, in this case with a strong focus on history and Near Eastern background, although there are many insightful theological comments as well. Harrison competently defends a traditionally orthodox approach to the book. However, he often addresses side issues rather than the real heart of the passage at hand. MS***

Levine, B. *Numbers 1–20.* AB. Doubleday, 1993. *Numbers 21–36.* AB. Doubleday, 2000. xvi/528 pp. and xxii/624 pp.

About Levine's erudition there is no doubt, and all serious students of Numbers must have this book. But Levine is not only convinced but also serious about his study of sources in the Book of Numbers. Those more concerned about the final form of the book will find the introductory material especially tedious. S****

Milgrom, J. *Numbers*. JPS Torah Commentary. Jewish Publication Society, 1990. lxi/520 pp.

This commentary is a masterpiece of erudition. The seventy-seven excurses are themselves worth the money. Milgrom gives the reader a careful study of the details and general message of the book. He is concerned to share the insights of medieval Jewish commentators, insights inaccessible to those who do not read postbiblical Hebrew. MS*****

Noordtzij, A. *Numbers*. BSC. Zondervan, 1983. ix/304 pp.

Originally published in Dutch in 1953, this commentary is particularly helpful in the area of theology. Other commentaries would be more helpful in the legal portions of Numbers. MS***

Olson, D. T. *Numbers*. Interp. John Knox, 1996. 196 pp.

No one has had a larger influence in recent years on our understanding of the theological theme of the book of Numbers than Olson. He exposits the book in the light of the theme of wilderness wandering and in the light of the structure formed by the two census accounts in chapters 1 and 26. Here we see judgment on the old generation of rebellion and the rise of the second generation of hope. He does reflect a traditionally critical view that the book essentially was composed after the exile and reflects the concerns of that time. LM*****

Philip, J. *Numbers*. CC. Word, 1987. 364 pp.

Philip is a prominent Scottish church leader who writes in an engaging style about the theology and significance of this rather neglected book. The commentary is backed by solid scholarship. Philip writes anecdotally, with the pastor primarily in mind. LM★★★★

Riggans, W. *Numbers.* DSB. Westminster, 1983. 252 pp.

Riggans does a good job relating the ancient biblical world to the modern one laypeople readily understand. He emphasizes the theological and practical aspects of Numbers. In keeping with the purpose of the series, he does not get much into introductory issues. LM★★★

Snaith, N. H. *Leviticus and Numbers.* NCB. Reprint, Sheffield, 1977.

See under Leviticus.

Wenham, G. J. *Numbers.* TOTC. Inter-Varsity, 1981. 240 pp.

Wenham does a wonderful job making this often neglected book come alive theologically. It is lamentable that the confines of the series have restricted the length of this commentary. Highly recommended for students, pastors, and scholars. LM★★★★

Deuteronomy

Brown, R. *The Message of Deuteronomy: Not by Bread Alone.* BST. Inter-Varsity, 1993. 331 pp.

This commentary, written by an English Baptist minister, is very helpful in its attempts to bridge the ancient text and modern social and ethical situations. It is not a deeply researched volume. It also adopts a rather topical theological approach to the text, which has its place, but it could have been much improved by a thematic, biblical-theological analysis. LM★★

Christensen, D. L. *Deuteronomy 1:1–21:9.* WBC. Nelson/ Paternoster, 2001. *Deuteronomy 21:10–34:12.* WBC. Nelson/Paternoster, 2002. cxii/458 pp. and li/440 pp.

Christensen first published a commentary on Deuteronomy 1–11 in this series, and the first volume, which covers 1:1–21:9, is a revision and expansion of that earlier work. This commentary is not for the timid. It is technical and also presents new theories about the nature of Deuteronomy. It is too early to call it idiosyncratic, but before the minister and student invests in this commentary over others that may be more helpful in terms of theological message, it is best to let scholars take a few years to sift through his ideas. The low rating reflects this fact and is clearly not a reflection on the author's obvious brilliance. MS**

Clifford, R. *Deuteronomy with Excursus on Covenant and Law.* OTM. Michael Glazier, 1982. 193 pp.

Clifford, well-known for his scholarly articles, dates the Book of Deuteronomy late and gives a two-hundred-year period of composition. He identifies the genre of the book as "speech modelled on covenant formulary" (3). The excursus is short but covers an important topic. Readable. LM***

Craigie, P. C. *The Book of Deuteronomy.* NICOT. Eerdmans, 1976. 424 pp.

Craigie is among the best of recent evangelical interpreters. His work on Deuteronomy is no exception to the high quality of his work. He is an astute theologian and philologist. He adopts a firmly evangelical approach to the Book of Deuteronomy, evident in his insistence on the essential unity of the book based on the treaty analogy. LM****

Cunliffe-Jones, H. *Deuteronomy.* TBC. SCM, 1951. 191 pp.

The author attempts to bring home to laypeople the complex issues surrounding the critical study of the book. He asserts that, since the book was written before Jesus Christ, "we must expect to find in it defects and distortions as well as true affirmations of faith." LM**

Driver, S. R. *A Critical and Exegetical Commentary on Deuteronomy.* 3d ed. ICC. T & T Clark, 1901. xcv/434 pp.

In many ways, this commentary is outdated. It retains its value because of Driver's ability as a philologist. Represents a turn-of-the-century critical view. S**

Maxwell, J. C. *Deuteronomy.* CC. Word, 1987. 351 pp.

The focus of this commentary is the relevance of Deuteronomy today. Of course, such a concern is admirable, but in this case it sometimes results in stretching the text's original purpose. Nonetheless, Maxwell's comments are usually on the mark. LM***

Mayes, A. D. H. *Deuteronomy.* NCB. Sheffield, 1979. 416 pp.

Shares some of the shortcomings of the series in that it comments on the RSV and is too brief. It is among the best, however, in the series. Comes from a critical perspective. LM***

McConville, J. G. *Deuteronomy.* Apollos Old Testament Commentary. Inter-Varsity, 2002. 544 pp.

McConville is one of the leading evangelical Old Testament scholars working today. He interacts extensively with the modern history of interpretation of the Book of Deuteronomy. The treatment is theologically sensitive. He provides a fresh approach to the book, an approach that needs serious consideration, although both conservatives and critics alike will find obstacles to acceptance. His writing is very accessible. MS*****

Merrill, E. H. *Deuteronomy.* NAC. Broadman, 1994. 477 pp.

This early contribution in the New American Commentary series is well-written and informative. It is particularly noteworthy in its consistent evangelical approach and in its thoroughgoing use of the covenant concept in the exposition of Deuteronomy. The scholarship on which it is based strikes one as a little dated. For instance, the use of the Hittite treaty form for early dating of the book (a conclusion with which I agree) does not take into account the flexible structure of the Hittite treaty itself. MS***

Miller, P. D., Jr. *Deuteronomy.* Interp. John Knox, 1990. xv/ 253 pp.

Miller is theologically concerned and sensitive to literary form in this helpful and well-written study. His approach is moderately critical, and his writing style is engaging. He deals with academic questions and cites previous studies, but his primary concern is with the meaning of the canonical text. M****

Payne, D. F. *Deuteronomy.* DSB. Westminster, 1985. 197 pp.

Payne writes clearly and nontechnically in this highly informative commentary. He divides the book into more than eighty sections and gives each a catchy title. This commentary remains open to the question of date. Nonetheless, it acknowledges that the book's message is especially relevant to times of political disaster. Payne examines Deuteronomy as a book of law, as a sermon, and as history. LM****

Ridderbos, J. *Deuteronomy.* BSC. 1950/51; Zondervan, 1984. 336 pp.

Ridderbos, one of the best Dutch Old Testament scholars of the previous generation, has contributed a formidable conservative defense against critical theories of Deuteronomy. He defends essential Mosaic authorship, while also recognizing the work of a later redactor. In the commentary proper, Ridderbos is theologically sensitive and exegetically insightful. He relates this Old Testament book to our New Testament situation. ML****

Thompson, J. A. *Deuteronomy.* TOTC. Inter-Varsity, 1974. 320 pp.

Although brief, this commentary is stimulating and full of helpful information. Thompson makes good use of the treaty analogy to Deuteronomy. He deals with many of the critical issues of the book from an evangelical perspective. Contains a thoughtful essay on the difficult question of the date of the book. Some good discussion of the theology of the book. LM****

Tigay, J. H. *Deuteronomy*. JPS Torah Commentary. Jewish Publication Society, 1996. xlix/548 pp.

A well-written and beautifully produced commentary that provides the Hebrew text, a translation, notes, and expository comments. The history of interpretation, particularly in Jewish tradition, is called upon to help elucidate the text. The approach to questions of history of composition is a moderately critical one. MS****

von Rad, G. *Deuteronomy*. OTL. Westminster/SCM, 1966. 211 pp.

Von Rad was one of the chief figures in Old Testament studies in the 1950s and beyond. He helped shape the method of study for the field during that time. This brief (especially considering the central importance of Deuteronomy to von Rad's research) commentary illustrates his approach and many of his most significant conclusions. His approach combines source, form, and redaction criticism. He concludes that while the final form of Deuteronomy is associated with Josiah's reform, the book was the product of northern Levites. S***

Weinfeld, M. *Deuteronomy 1–11*. AB. Doubleday, 1991. xiv/448 pp.

The first volume of Weinfeld's commentary illustrates his erudition and insight into this biblical book. Deuteronomy's first eleven chapters, Weinfeld writes, contain history and sermon; the rest of Deuteronomy concentrates on law and will be the focus of the second volume. All the introductory material is found in the first volume (with exception of discussion of text). Weinfeld writes from a critical point of view, believing that much of the material in Deuteronomy is ancient, but that it received a major redaction during the Hezekiah and Josiah reforms. There is much interesting literary and theological discussion surrounding the relationship between the book and covenant/loyalty oaths. MS*****

Wright, C. K. *Deuteronomy.* NIBCOT. Hendrickson/Paternoster, 1996. 350 pp.

Wright, a well-known biblical ethicist, does well with the Book of Deuteronomy with a special emphasis on his area of expertise and interest. He has a refreshing belief in a "substantial Mosaic legacy" of the book. He is sensitive to the book's trajectory to the New Testament. LM****

Joshua

Auld, A. G. *Joshua, Judges, and Ruth.* DSB. Westminster, 1984. 290 pp.

A short but insightful and extremely readable exposition. In a brief introduction, Auld expresses a skeptical view concerning historicity, but his theological sensitivities redeem the volume. LM***

Boling, R. G., and G. E. Wright. *Joshua.* AB. Doubleday, 1982. xvii/580 pp.

Wright's untimely death prevented his full participation in this project; most of the work is that of his well-known student Boling (who also did the Judges commentary for this series). The commentary is critical in its approach to the text and theology of Joshua. The history and archaeology of Israel are emphasized. MS**

Butler, T. *Joshua.* WBC. Nelson/Paternoster, 1983. xliii/304 pp.

A well-researched and thought-through commentary. Full of philological, textual, and exegetical information and insight. An evangelical, but not traditional, viewpoint on the book. MS****

Goslinga, C. J. *Joshua, Judges, Ruth.* BSC. Zondervan, 1986. 558 pp.

This commentary was translated from a Dutch original that dates from the late 1920s and early 1930s. Although it may not take into account the most recent scholarship, it is an excellent commentary from an evangelical-Reformed standpoint. Strong on theology. MS***

Gray, J. *Joshua, Judges, and Ruth.* NCB. 1967; rev. ed., Sheffield/Marshall Pickering, 1986. 427 pp.

Follows Noth in attributing both Joshua and Judges to the Deuteronomist (and assumes a seventh-century date for Deuteronomy). Gray believes that Joshua is of limited value as a historical work. He believes that Judges is a more sober account of history. S*

Hamlin, E. J. *Joshua: Inheriting the Land.* ITC. Handsel, 1983. xxiii/207 pp.

This is an engagingly written exposition of Joshua that looks at the book as a continuation of the exodus pattern. Hamlin examines the conquest in the light of the theme of the liberation of the oppressed and asks how the text is relevant for today. The book imbibes of a moderate historical criticism to make its point. M***

Harris, J. G., C. Brown, and M. Moore. *Joshua, Judges, Ruth.* NIBCOT. Hendrickson/Paternoster, 2000. xxxiii/398 pp.

Though the authors of the three parts of the book are different they are aligned in their "canonical historical approach" to their subject matter, with good results. LM***

Hess, R. S. *Joshua.* TOTC. Inter-Varsity, 1996. 320 pp.

This is one of the best TOTC commentaries and one of the best on the Book of Joshua. Hess, an acknowledged expert on ancient Near Eastern literature and Israelite history, defends the essential authenticity of the historical memory of the book. He also is an adept interpreter of the literary and theological aspects of the book. LM*****

Hoppe, L. *Joshua, Judges*. OTM. Michael Glazier, 1982.

A popularly oriented theological study of the final form of the text. Hoppe helpfully orients his readers to the concept of the Deuteronomic history. He is less successful in dealing with the important theological concept of holy war. LM**

Howard, D. M., Jr. *Joshua*. NAC. Broadman, 1998. 464 pp.

This commentary is one of the best on Joshua, though the field is not particularly strong. Nonetheless, Howard's contribution is well-written, well-researched, and well-thought-out. He adopts a relatively conservative approach to the history that is particularly admirable in this age of skepticism. He is also quite good at pointing out theological themes. LM****

Huffman, J. A., Jr. *Joshua*. CC. Word, 1986. 282 pp.

Huffman follows the format of the series to a tee. He effectively relates the book to modern lay concerns. By use of anecdote and illustration, Huffman stimulates thinking about how to communicate the book's message. It is important, however, to use this commentary with a more content-oriented commentary at hand. LM***

Madvig, D. H. *Joshua*. EBC 3. Zondervan, 1992.

This commentary is a good, basic retelling of the biblical story, filling in some of the gaps. Not a lot of theological reflection. LM**

Miller, J. M., and G. M. Tucker. *The Book of Joshua*. CBC. Cambridge University Press, 1974. x/206 pp.

The authors give a careful description of the literary composition of the book from a critical perspective. They concentrate on the Deuteronomistic redaction, which they think is the strongest voice in the book. They exaggerate supposed contradictions in the book and use archaeology to inform their commentary. LM**

Nelson, R. *Joshua*. OTL. Westminster John Knox, 1997. xviii/310 pp.

Nelson has a low view of the historical worth of the book. Employs both diachronic as well as synchronic analyses, but the commentary has a kind of "old school" critical feel. S**

Soggin, J. *Joshua*. OTL. Westminster, 1972. xvii/245 pp.

Soggin, an Italian scholar writing in the German tradition, emphasizes historical and archaeological studies. Not much theological comment. S**

Woudstra, M. *The Book of Joshua*. NICOT. Eerdmans, 1981. xiv/396 pp.

Woudstra gives a very good exegetical analysis of the book. He also has an excellent biblical-theological sense. There are some good literary observations, but much more could be done in this area. LM***

Judges

Auld, A. G. *Joshua, Judges, and Ruth*. DSB. Westminster, 1984.

See under Joshua.

Block, D. I. *Judges, Ruth*. NAC. Broadman, 1999. 765 pp.

This substantial contribution is clearly the best thing available on the Book of Judges. Block is thoroughly aware of all the literature that precedes him, and he incorporates what is good and criticizes what is bad. His own perspective may be idiosyncratic on rare occasions, but it is usually very insightful. This commentary is particularly strong in literary and theological analysis. LM*****

Boling, R. G. *Judges*. AB. Doubleday, 1975. xxi/338 pp.

This volume is perhaps one of the most well-known recent commentaries on the Book of Judges. It is competently written from a critical perspective with an emphasis on history, comparative studies, and philology. Boling suggests a peasant-revolt model of the conquest and believes that Israel's early social structure is similar to Greek amphictyonies. He also utilizes the covenant-treaty analogy. There is not much in the way of literary or theological reflection, as is typical of the series. MS***

Cundall, A. E., and L. Morris. *Judges and Ruth.* TOTC. Inter-Varsity, 1968. 318 pp.

Cundall's section on Judges is an adequate, but not outstanding, treatment of that book. He argues for a conservative position on the historicity of Judges and Joshua, believing the two books give complementary, and not contradictory, perspectives on the conquest. LM**

Goslinga, C. J. *Joshua, Judges, Ruth.* BSC. Zondervan, 1986.

See under Joshua.

Gray, J. *Joshua, Judges, and Ruth.* NCB. Sheffield, 1967.

See under Joshua.

Hamlin, E. J. *Judges: At Risk in the Promised Land.* ITC. Handsel, 1990. xii/182 pp.

Hamlin applies a rather idiosyncratic critical approach to the Book of Judges, following the method of N. Gottwald's *The Tribes of Yahweh.* The commentary provides no philological or text-critical information, but nonetheless Hamlin concentrates on theology and application. Some of his attempts to bridge from the ancient text to the modern situation seem forced, such as when he connects the Israelites living in caves (Judg. 6:2) to modern slum conditions. LM**

Harris, J. G., C. Brown, and M. Moore. *Joshua, Judges, Ruth.* NIBCOT. Hendrickson/Paternoster, 2000. 398 pp.

See under Joshua.

Lewis, A. H. *Judges/Ruth.* EBC. Moody, 1979. 128 pp.

Lewis writes on a popular level and in a devotional vein. He does integrate some scholarly material and uses archaeological information. LM**

Martin, J. D. *The Book of Judges*. CBC. Cambridge University Press, 1975. x/234 pp.

This commentary is a concise statement of current critical theory on the Book of Judges. Martin is historically skeptical. For instance, he connects the Samson stories with sun mythology. LM**

Moore, G. F. *A Critical and Exegetical Commentary on Judges*. ICC. T & T Clark, 1895. 476 pp.

Like the other volumes in this series, Moore's commentary is critical and highly technical. S**

Soggin, J. A. *Judges*. OTL. Westminster/SCM, 1981. xx/305 pp.

Once again, as in his commentary on Joshua, Soggin concentrates on critical and historical issues. He consciously avoids making theological statements. However, this is a more mature and profitable commentary than his earlier commentary on Joshua. S***

Wilcock, M. *The Message of Judges: Grace Abounding*. BST. Inter-Varsity, 1992. 175 pp.

Wilcock provides an interesting retelling of the story of Judges. He makes the story come alive for the lay reader and also derives moral and behavioral principles from the book. This is not the commentary for technical information about the book, and it is not particularly satisfying for theological meditation. LM***

Wolf, H. *Judges*. EBC 3. Zondervan, 1992.

Very competent and well-written. But once again, in keeping with the series, not especially profound. LM***

Younger, K. L., Jr. *Judges/Ruth*. NIVAC. Zondervan/Hodder & Stoughton, 2002. 511 pp.

See under Ruth.

Ruth

Atkinson, D. *The Message of Ruth: The Wings of Refuge*. BST. Inter-Varsity, 1983. 128 pp.

Atkinson is an interesting writer here as he is in his Genesis 1–11 commentary. He gives some stimulating illustrations as he exposits the major themes of the book. He focuses on providence. LM***

Auld, A. G. *Joshua, Judges, and Ruth.* DSB. Westminster, 1984.

See under Joshua.

Block, D. I. *Judges, Ruth.* NAC. Broadman, 1999. 765 pp.

See under Judges.

Bush, R. W. *Ruth/Esther.* WBC. Nelson/Paternoster, 1996. xiv/514 pp.

See under Esther.

Campbell, E. F., Jr. *Ruth.* AB. Doubleday, 1975. xx/189 pp.

This is a very stimulating and well-written commentary. Campbell explores many of the ancient social conventions that lie behind the text (levirate marriage, the kinsman redeemer, the removal of the sandal). He provides an early example of literary analysis. MS***

Cundall, A. E., and L. Morris. *Judges and Ruth.* TOTC. Inter-Varsity, 1968.

See under Judges. Morris, a New Testament scholar, comments on Ruth. He shows a good knowledge of the Old Testament and its background. LM**

Fuerst, W. J. *The Books of Ruth, Esther, Ecclesiastes, the Song of Songs, Lamentations.* CBC. Cambridge University Press, 1975. x/267 pp.

These five books are grouped together since each has a place in one of the five major Jewish festivals. Fuerst provides a helpful, although somewhat critical, approach to these books. LM***

Goslinga, C. J. *Joshua, Judges, Ruth.* BSC. Zondervan, 1986.

See under Joshua.

Gray, J. *Joshua, Judges, and Ruth.* NCB. Sheffield, 1967. See under Joshua.

Harris, J. G., C. Brown, and M. Moore. *Joshua, Judges, Ruth.* NIBCOT. Hendrickson/Paternoster, 2000. 398 pp. See under Joshua.

Hubbard, R. L., Jr. *The Book of Ruth.* NICOT. Eerdmans, 1988. xiv/317 pp.

This commentary's introduction is extensive and profitable as it discusses issues of unity, theology, canonicity, text, and more. The commentary as a whole demonstrates careful scholarship, a lively writing style, and balanced judgment. Hubbard pays attention to all aspects of the Book of Ruth. This commentary is one of the very best of the series. MS*****

Huey, F. B., Jr. *Ruth.* EBC 3. Zondervan, 1992.

Well-written and interesting at times, but once again (for this series), nothing really beyond the basics. LM***

Knight, G. A. F. *Ruth and Jonah.* TBC. SCM, 1950. 93 pp.

These two books are surprisingly treated together on the principle that they both deal with the postexilic problem of how to live with those outside of ethnic boundaries and, as opposed to Ezra, how to take a tolerant stand. LM**

Murphy, R. E. *Wisdom Literature: Job, Proverbs, Ruth, Canticles, Ecclesiastes, and Esther.* FOTL. Eerdmans, 1981. 185 pp.

See under Job.

Nielsen, Kirsten. *Ruth.* OTL. Westminster John Knox/ SCM, 1997. xiv/106 pp.

Generically, Nielsen believes that Ruth, with its connection between narrative and genealogy, is most like the patriarchal narratives. She employs intertextuality and analyzes Ruth's use of earlier biblical tradition. In particular, she finds the story of Tamar in Genesis 38 especially illuminating. She presents an interesting description of her hermeneutical theory in the introduction. The intention of Ruth is to counter a smear campaign against David that shows he is descended from a Moabite, but the book shows that this is all the will of Yahweh. MS***

Sakenfeld, K. D. *Ruth*. Interp. John Knox, 1999. xii/91pp.

Though a relatively short commentary—even for a short book like Ruth—Sakenfeld has provided a great deal of insight into both the theological and sociological significance of the book. LM****

Sasson, J. M. *Ruth: A New Translation with a Philological Commentary and a Formalist-Folklorist Interpretation.* 2d ed. JSOT, 1989. xviii/292 pp.

This major scholarly study needs to be consulted on philological matters. Sasson shows great literary sensitivity, depending on V. Propp for formal analysis. The commentary is a repository of discussion on the book. S****

Younger, K. L., Jr. *Judges/Ruth*. NIVAC. Zondervan/Hodder & Stoughton, 2002. 511 pp.

Younger is an insightful and learned student of the Old Testament, and he does a good job in particular with the "original meaning" section of the commentary. He describes well Ruth's historical background, literary devices, and theological message. He is often insightful, but not as strong on the "contemporary significance" of the book. LM****

Samuel

Ackroyd, P. R. *The First Book of Samuel.* CBC. Cambridge University Press, 1977. *The Second Book of Samuel.* CBC. Cambridge University Press, 1977. 238 pp. and xii/ 247 pp.

Although his expertise is in the Persian period, Ackroyd is one of the best English biblical scholars of the generation and produces a competent critical commentary on 1 Samuel. He writes clearly and for a popular audience. He is skeptical about the historicity of the book. LM***

Anderson, A. A. *2 Samuel.* WBC. Nelson/Paternoster, 1989. xl/302 pp.

This commentary is thoroughly researched and meticulously presented. Anderson does a good job presenting the critical issues of the book and also expressing his own moderately critical perspective. He does an especially good job dealing with the important text-critical problem of the book. The bibliographies are well-done. A number of unfortunate typographical errors can be found. MS****

Arnold, B. T. *1 and 2 Samuel.* NIVAC. Zondervan, 2003. 681 pp.

Within the space constraints of the series, Arnold's treatment of the original meaning is illuminating. It cannot go into the depth of the more purely scholarly series, but most readers will find the treatment more than adequate. What Arnold's volume has that the others do not are very helpful trajectories from the ancient text to today's church and society. Arnold writes in a clear and accessible style. LM****

Baldwin, J. *1 and 2 Samuel.* TOTC. Inter-Varsity, 1988. 299 pp.

Baldwin's commentary is characterized by careful and up-to-date scholarship. She writes with the educated lay reader in mind. In the introduction, she critiques some critical theories of composition (Wellhausen and Noth). She leaves the question up in the air, since the biblical material is not specific. The emphasis of the commentary is on exegesis and theology. LM****

Bergen, R. D. *1, 2 Samuel.* NAC. Broadman, 1996. 416 pp.

Competent and readable treatment of the narrative of Samuel. Sensitive to historical, literary, and theological issues. LM***

Brueggemann, W. *First and Second Samuel.* Interp. John Knox, 1990. x/362 pp.

Brueggemann, who produced the highly regarded Genesis commentary in this series, has produced a fascinating study of Samuel. His writing style is not just engaging but also exciting. He is a moderate critic who takes a canonical approach to the text. LM****

Chafin, K. L. *1, 2 Samuel.* CC. Word, 1989. 404 pp.

Chafin devotes more space than is typical in this series to the interpretation and explanation of the biblical text. He also uses the anecdotal style that characterizes the other volumes. He has a good grasp of the text, although (as with the series as a whole) he would benefit from a healthy dose of biblical theology. LM***

Conroy, C. *1–2 Samuel; 1–2 Kings, with an Excursus on Davidic Dynasty and Holy City Zion.* OTM. Michael Glazier, 1983. 266 pp.

Conroy has written competently on a scholarly level on Samuel before doing this commentary. He is sensitive to the book as literature. He has an excursus on David and Zion in the Old Testament, but could have developed the New Testament connections more extensively. LM***

Evans, M. J. *1 and 2 Samuel.* NIBCOT. Hendrickson/Paternoster, 2000. xiv/267 pp.

Her analysis of Samuel focuses on the role of power, its "nature, accession, use, and abuse" (9). She has a good literary sense, particularly in her analysis of the plot and characterization of the narrative. LM***

Gordon, R. P. *1 and 2 Samuel.* Zondervan, 1988. 375 pp.

This commentary is a refreshing literary reading of Samuel. It is full of good theological insight and occasional philological and textual comments. MS****

Hertzberg, H. W. *I and II Samuel.* OTL. Westminster/SCM, 1964. 416 pp.

A good exegetical commentary from a critical perspective. Not much theological help. MS***

Jobling, D. *1 Samuel.* Berit Olam. Michael Glazier, 1998. x/330 pp.

This commentary is written from a postmodern, eclectic standpoint. The best use of this book is to read it to see how such a hermeneutic influences one's reading rather than to use it for exploring the meaning of Samuel. MS***

Klein, R. W. *I Samuel.* WBC. Nelson/Paternoster, 1983. xxxiii/307 pp.

This commentary is particularly helpful as a guide to the text-critical, philological, and historical issues of 1 Samuel. Textual issues are particularly important for this book. Klein has chosen not to concentrate on literary or theological issues, and this choice weakens the commentary. MS****

McCarter, P. Kyle, Jr. *I Samuel.* AB. Doubleday, 1980. *II Samuel.* AB. Doubleday, 1984. xii/475 pp. and xviii/553 pp.

McCarter is the most competent text critic to deal with Samuel, although in his conclusions Klein is probably better since he tends to stick with the MT more often (and this appears warranted by the evidence). McCarter, however, had access to the Dead Sea Scrolls of Samuel. Although written from a critical perspective, this commentary is well worth having. MS****

Mauchline, J. *1 and 2 Samuel.* NCB. Sheffield, 1971. 336 pp.

Mauchline's commentary suffers from the limits of this series. It is a commentary on the RSV and too short. Of very little help. S*

Miscall, P. D. *I Samuel: A Literary Reading.* Indiana University Press, 1986. xxv/198 pp.

In approach, this commentary is to be compared most

closely with that of Gordon. In such a comparison, Gordon's comes out on top. This assessment is based on the literary approach applied. Miscall advocates a kind of deconstructionist heightening of the gaps of the narrative, while Gordon applies a new-critical close reading. This volume can help if consulted, but it is not necessary for an individual's reference library. MS★★

Payne, D. F. *I and II Samuel.* DSB. Westminster, 1982. viii/ 278 pp.

Payne's style is very accessible, in the tradition of DSB. He makes ancient customs understandable and emphasizes a theological exposition. He identifies the leading theme of First and Second Samuel as leadership—a theme that anticipates Christ. LM★★★

Smith, H. P. *Samuel.* ICC. T & T Clark, 1899. xxxix/421 pp.

Although less so than other volumes in the series, this commentary is highly technical and not easy to read. It imbibes the same optimistic critical attitude of other biblical studies at the end of the nineteenth century. Smith spends considerable time delineating sources and contradictory teachings within the book. S★★

Youngblood, R. F. *1, 2 Samuel.* EBC 3. Zondervan, 1992.

Youngblood's commentary on Samuel justifies purchasing the third EBC volume. It takes up half the book and is clearly the most mature of the entries. The author gives a balanced assessment of both the book's content as well as the secondary literature, with which he interacts with profit. LM★★★★

Kings

Auld, A. G. *Kings.* DSB. Westminster, 1986. 259 pp.

Auld gives a clear, simple exposition of the text. He emphasizes meaning and application. LM★★★

Brueggemann, W. *1 and 2 Kings.* SHBC. Smyth and Helwys, 2000. 645 pp.

Brueggemann is always interesting and insightful and this, the inaugural volume in a new series, does not disappoint. Brueggemann is always asking questions that are relevant to church and society today. An easy read and even a commentary series with illustrations! LM****

Cogan, M. *I Kings*. AB. Doubleday, 2001. xvii/556 pp.

Cogan along with H. Tadmor produced the volume on 2 Kings twelve years before. This volume is Cogan's alone and includes the introduction to the whole promised in the earlier volume. Like the previous contribution, this one also emphasizes history and ancient Near Eastern background but is also sensitive to literary qualities. Especially interesting is his discussion in the introduction of sources of Kings. MS****

Cogan, M., and H. Tadmor. *II Kings*. AB. Doubleday, 1988. xxxv/371 pp.

Cogan and Tadmor are historically oriented experts in Mesopotamian studies. Thus it is not surprising that they concentrate on the Mesopotamian historical backdrop of the book. S****

DeVries, S. *I Kings*. WBC. Nelson/Paternoster, 1985. lxiv/286 pp.

DeVries takes a traditionally critical approach to the Book of Kings. He is heavy on source, form, and redaction criticism. These critical methods have an important function to play if used correctly. Unfortunately, they are abused here. Very little theological or exegetical insight. S**

Dilday, R. H., Jr. *1, 2 Kings*. CC. Word, 1987. 512 pp.

This is not one of the stronger volumes in the series. It would have been much better had the introduction been expanded to include an extensive discussion of the book's theological purpose and sermonic tone. As it is, the commentary tends to be moralistic. LM**

Gray, J. *I and II Kings*. OTL. Westminster/SCM, 1963. 744 pp.

This has been the classic commentary on Kings for the past forty years. Gray presents especially detailed work on chronology and sources from a critical perspective. There is not much theological commentary. S***

Hobbs, T. R. *2 Kings.* WBC. Nelson/Paternoster, 1985. xlviii/ 388 pp.

A well-written and insightful commentary. Its helpful methodological presupposition is that 2 Kings is the work of one author. Hobbs utilizes the literary approach to great benefit. MS****

House, P. R. *1, 2 Kings.* NAC. Broadman, 1995. 432 pp.

The introduction to the commentary gives an excellent and clear exposition of the issues surrounding the interpretation of the book. House gives a good résumé of the secondary literature as well as his own ideas. In particular, he argues that a major theological theme of the book is the presentation and protection of monotheism. LM****

Hubbard, R. L., Jr. *First and Second Kings.* EBC. Moody, 1991. 240 pp.

Hubbard gives us an excellent popular commentary on this most interesting of historical books. He provides a very helpful entry into the theological significance of this recounting of Israel's past. The introduction would have been helped by further exploration of the relationship between Kings and Deuteronomy. LM****

Jones, G. H. *1 and 2 Kings.* 2 vols. NCB. Sheffield, 1985. lii/ 666 pp.

This two-volume commentary is one of the best in the series. In the first place, the commentary is proportionally longer than most volumes in NCB, allowing for fuller comment. Jones has a more extensive introduction and bibliography, which also increases the commentary's value. LM***

Long, B. O. *I Kings with an Introduction to Historical Literature.* FOTL. Eerdmans, 1984. xv/265 pp.

Long provides a thoughtful study of the Book of Kings and the nature of Israelite historiographical literature from a critical theological perspective. It is particularly gratifying that he is attuned to contemporary literary theory. From an evangelical point of view, his view of the historicity of the text is low. S***

Montgomery, J. A., and J. S. Gehman. *Kings*. ICC. T & T Clark, 1951. xlvii/575 pp.

Montgomery's commentary was originally scheduled for publication more than a decade before it appeared but was delayed by the war. Due to his death in 1949, it fell to his student, Gehman, to put the work in final form. Montgomery's contribution, in keeping with the nature of the series, is extremely erudite and technical. He concentrates in the introduction on textual criticism, issues of composition, chronology, and the nature of historiography. S***

Nelson, R. *First and Second Kings*. Interp. John Knox, 1987. 252 pp.

In keeping with the series, Nelson, a respected scholar on Kings, concentrates on theology and literature, not history. Among other things, he emphasizes the connection with the world of Deuteronomy. He writes in a vivid and engaging style. M****

Provan, I. W. *1 and 2 Kings*. NIBCOT. Hendrickson/Paternoster, 1995. xiv/306 pp.

This is certainly in its perspective and readability the best available commentary on Kings. The writing is very accessible, and the emphasis is on literary and theological issues, though the notes also address particular exegetical issues. Too bad that, in keeping with the series, the treatment is necessarily brief. LM*****

Rice, G. *I Kings: Nations under God*. ITC. Handsel, 1990. xv/198 pp.

This commentary is a well-written narrative retelling the story of 1 Kings. Rice provides a unit-by-unit exposition with theological reflections sprinkled throughout. Faithful and occasionally insightful. LM***

Robinson, J. *The First Book of Kings*. CBC. Cambridge University Press, 1972. *The Second Book of Kings*. CBC. Cambridge University Press, 1976. xi/259 pp. and xi/256 pp.

Robinson gives a concise summary of the historical background of the book. He connects its composition with the Deuteronomic reform. He writes in an easy-to-read style. Moderately critical. LM***

Walsh, J. T. *1 Kings*. Berit Olam. Michael Glazier, 1996. xxi/393 pp.

Walsh provides a narrative reading of 1 Kings. He brackets issues of history and retells the biblical story with the aid of recent insights into the conventions of biblical storytelling. Sometimes the commentary is more like a paraphrase of the biblical account. At other times, interesting insight into the text is provided. LM***

Wiseman, D. J. *1 and 2 Kings*. TOTC. Inter-Varsity, 1993. 318 pp.

D. J. Wiseman is greatly appreciated for his important work on ancient Near Eastern literature and for his interest in archaeology. These interests are emphasized in his analysis of Kings and are a tremendous strength of the volume. However, Wiseman is not as interested nor as incisive a commentator on the theological and literary aspects of the text. LM***

Chronicles

Allen, L. C. *1, 2 Chronicles*. CC. Word, 1987. 445 pp.

This is an excellent volume for laypeople, pastors, and other Christian leaders. There is deep research behind this well-written volume. LM****

Braun, R. *1 Chronicles*. WBC. Nelson/Paternoster, 1986. xlv/311 pp.

A very helpful discussion of all aspects of the book. Good bibliographies, sensitive exegesis, and helpful comments on Old Testament theology. MS****

Curtis, E. L. *Chronicles.* ICC. T & T Clark, 1910. xxii/534 pp.

Curtis has a low view of Chronicles' historical value. He believes it is unhistorical. He does not prize Chronicles' priestly theology. He does provide a scholarly and extensive discussion of the text of Chronicles, but this is dated. S*

DeVries, S. *1 and 2 Chronicles.* FOTL. Eerdmans, 1989. xv/ 439 pp.

As with the other commentaries in the series, DeVries concentrates on the structure, genre, and intention of the book. This volume is up to date and provides a good perspective on contemporary scholarly opinion on Chronicles. The bibliographies are of special value. S***

Dillard, R. B. *II Chronicles.* WBC. Nelson/Paternoster, 1987. xxiii/323 pp.

This commentary makes 2 Chronicles come alive. It is superb in its analysis of the theological message, given Second Chronicles' composition in the postexilic period. It is one of the few OT commentaries that explores connections with the New Testament. MS*****

Japhet, S. *I and II Chronicles.* OTL. Westminster John Knox/ SCM, 1993. xxv/1,077 pp.

This masterful commentary covers the bases on the Book of Chronicles: philology, text, literary strategy, and history. Its weakest point is theology. But this commentary is a must for all serious students. There is extensive discussion of the secondary literature. Japhet is critical in her thinking, but moderately so, and she arrives at a number of relatively conservative conclusions. MS*****

McConville, J. G. *I and II Chronicles.* DSB. Westminster, 1984. 280 pp.

This commentary is an interesting and solid exposition of an often-neglected book. McConville is sensitive to theology and application. LM****

Myers, J. M. *1 and 2 Chronicles.* 2 vols. AB. Doubleday, 1965. xciv/241 pp. and 267 pp.

Myers concentrates on issues of history and text. Of very little help in the area of theology. Recent commentaries are much better. S**

Selman, M. J. *1 Chronicles.* TOTC. Inter-Varsity, 1994. *2 Chronicles.* TOTC. Inter-Varsity, 1994. 263 pp. and 286 pp.

Though the whole commentary is relatively short for a book (in two parts) of this size, the introduction is lengthy and helpful. Selman presents a strong case for why the Book of Chronicles makes an important contribution to the canon. LM****

Thompson, J. A. *1, 2 Chronicles.* NAC. Broadman, 1994. 410 pp.

A competent, easy-to-read study of Chronicles with an emphasis on the theological meaning of the book. However, compared to Braun, Dillard, Williamson, and others, there is not much new or exciting here. LM***

Tuell, S. S. *First and Second Chronicles.* Interp. Westminster John Knox, 2001. xii/252 pp.

Tuell believes that Chronicles is an "extended meditation on the Hebrew scriptures" (7) with an emphasis on David and the worship in the temple. One of the important messages of Chronicles is to encourage the study of scripture as that which brings divine blessing. LM***

Wilcock, M. *The Message of Chronicles: One Church, One Faith, One Lord.* BST. Inter-Varsity, 1987. 288 pp.

Wilcock's popular commentary on Chronicles makes much of the fact that the biblical book is sermonic history. Wilcock's writing style is good, and he competently brings out the ancient text's message for today. LM****

Williamson, H. G. M. *1 and 2 Chronicles*. NCB. Sheffield, 1982. xix/428 pp.

In spite of the limitations of the series, this is a very good commentary. Williamson is a well-known expert in postexilic matters and brings his formidable knowledge to bear on the text of Chronicles. MS★★★★

Ezra

Batten, L. W. *Ezra and Nehemiah*. ICC. T & T Clark, 1913. xv/384 pp.

Batten represents the best of turn-of-the-century critical scholarship. He argues that Ezra–Nehemiah comes from the same school as Chronicles. Occasionally, he attempts to undo what he calls "the mischief of the Redactor" by transposing verses. S★★

Blenkinsopp, J. *Ezra–Nehemiah*. OTL. Westminster/SCM, 1988. 366 pp.

Blenkinsopp is one of the leading scholars of the postexilic period, and his erudition comes to the fore in this excellent volume. He informs the reader of contemporary scholarship, but does not always agree with the current opinion (see, for instance, his view on the relation of these books to the Chronicler). He also asserts the need for diachronic analysis as well as a more literary or canonical approach. MS★★★★

Breneman, M. *Ezra, Nehemiah, Esther*. NAC. Broadman, 1993. 383 pp.

Breneman has produced a competent and readable commentary on these three short and late biblical books. He gives good, simple descriptions of the historical backgrounds of the story. A popular presentation of some of the most important scholarly decisions on the book. LM★★★

Brockington, L. H. *Ezra, Nehemiah, and Esther*. NCB. Sheffield, 1969. 189 pp.

Brockington's introduction displays a typical critical approach to the book. His comments on the text are sparse, as is usual in this series. MS**

Clines, D. J. A. *Ezra, Nehemiah, Esther.* NCB. Sheffield, 1984. 342 pp.

In his typical manner, Clines presents a carefully and thoroughly researched commentary. His writing is both scholarly and clear. He carefully presents the important and debated issues of historical background. There is also an excellent study of Esther's historicity. LM****

Coggins, R. J. *The Books of Ezra and Nehemiah.* CBC. Cambridge University Press, 1976. xi/150 pp.

Coggins presents a concise, simple, critical perspective. He argues for a close connection between the Chronicler and Ezra–Nehemiah. He notes some historical problems. LM***

Fensham, F. C. *The Books of Ezra and Nehemiah.* NICOT. Eerdmans, 1982. xiii/288 pp.

This commentary is traditional in its approach to these two books. For instance, it accepts the view that Ezra arrived in Palestine in 458 B.C. before Nehemiah, who arrived in 445 B.C. Fensham further argues that the Chronicler was responsible for both Ezra and Nehemiah. The emphasis of this volume is on history and culture, but other aspects, like philology and theology, are treated as well. MS****

Holmgren, F. C. *Ezra and Nehemiah: Israel Alive Again.* ITC. Handsel, 1987. xvii/167 pp.

This is a theological enquiry into Ezra–Nehemiah with an eye toward their significance for today. It presents a moderately critical approach. It is easy and stimulating to read. LM***

Kidner, D. *Ezra and Nehemiah.* TOTC. Inter-Varsity, 1979. 174 pp.

This volume is similar in approach to the Fensham commentary, but much less scholarly in tone (although the scholarship is there to back it up). It is thus easy to read and emphasizes theology and history. LM****

McConville, J. G. *Ezra, Nehemiah, and Esther.* DSB. Westminster, 1985. xii/197 pp.

This volume is readable and scholarly without being overly academic. McConville is excellent at both revealing the books' meaning in their Old Testament context and explaining their relevance for today. LM****

Myers, J. M. *Ezra, Nehemiah.* AB. Doubleday, 1965. lxxxiii/267 pp.

Myers concentrates on a critical reconstruction of the time period reflected in these two books. The commentary is weak in the areas of philology, literary structure, style, and theology. S*

Throntveit, M. A. *Ezra–Nehemiah.* Interp. John Knox, 1992. xiii/129 pp.

This easy-to-read yet profound commentary takes full advantage of recent work on these two biblical books without bogging down the reader in too many footnotes. It emphasizes and combines literary analysis and theological message, while downplaying the historical issues of the book. Avoids a typical moralistic reading of the book as well. LM****

Williamson, H. G. M. *Ezra–Nehemiah.* WBC. Nelson/Paternoster, 1985. xix/428 pp.

This is a comprehensive, scholarly commentary written by a highly competent evangelical scholar. Williamson is a lecturer at Cambridge University, and his research specialty is postexilic literature. Although scholarly, this book is helpful to laypeople as well. MS*****

Nehemiah

Blenkinsopp, J. *Ezra–Nehemiah.* OTL. Westminster, 1988. 366 pp.

See under Ezra.

Breneman, M. *Ezra, Nehemiah, Esther.* NAC. Broadman, 1993. 383 pp.
See under Ezra.

Brockington, L. H. *Ezra, Nehemiah, and Esther.* NCB. Sheffield, 1969. 189 pp.
See under Ezra.

Holmgren, F. C. *Ezra and Nehemiah: Israel Alive Again.* ITC. Handsel, 1987. xvii/167 pp.
See under Ezra.

Kidner, D. *Ezra and Nehemiah.* TOTC. Inter-Varsity, 1979. 174 pp.
See under Ezra.

McConville, J. G. *Ezra, Nehemiah and Esther.* DSB. Westminster, 1985. xii/197 pp.
See under Ezra.

Myers, J. M. *Ezra, Nehemiah.* AB. Doubleday, 1965. lxxxiii/267 pp.
See under Ezra.

Williamson, H. G. M. *Ezra–Nehemiah.* WBC. Nelson/Paternoster, 1985. xix/428 pp.
See under Ezra.

Esther

Baldwin, J. G. *Esther.* TOTC. Inter-Varsity, 1984. 126 pp.

Baldwin combines a keen literary and theological sense with a firm and intelligent opinion concerning the book's historicity. The commentary is well-written and based upon thorough research. LM****

Breneman, M. *Ezra, Nehemiah, Esther.* NAC. Broadman, 1993. 383 pp.
See under Ezra.

Brockington, L. H. *Ezra, Nehemiah, and Esther.* NCB. Sheffield, 1969.

See under Ezra.

Bush, R. W. *Ruth/Esther.* WBC. Nelson/Paternoster, 1996. xiv/514 pp.

This is one of the most extensive commentaries written on these two short books. It is very competent, but tends to be a bit technical. Bush is particularly good at philology. He gives a thorough discussion of all the technical issues. MS*****

Coggins, R. J., and S. P. Re'emi. *Nahum, Obadiah, Esther: Israel among the Nations.* ITC. Handsel, 1985.

See under Obadiah.

Jobes, K. *Esther.* NIVAC. Zondervan/Hodder & Stoughton, 1999. 248 pp.

Without a doubt this is the best commentary to buy on Esther. It is informative about its original meaning and insightful on how to apply it to the contemporary world. Jobes is theologically astute and a good writer. LM*****

Levenson, J. D. *Esther.* OTL. John Knox/SCM, 1997. xvi/142 pp.

This commentary provides a readable and often interesting interpretation of Esther that also is well-versed in the ancient and modern scholarly literature. It also pays attention to the Greek version of the story that is significantly different from the Hebrew version and that is accepted by Catholics as authoritative. Levenson believes that Esther seems well-aware of authentic Persian customs and history, but in the final analysis believes it is a work of historical fiction. MS****

McConville, J. G. *Ezra, Nehemiah, and Esther.* DSB. Westminster, 1985. xii/197 pp.

See under Ezra.

Moore, C. A. *Esther.* AB. Doubleday, 1971. xiv/118 pp.

A competent commentary on the book from a nonevangelical perspective. There is a lengthy introductory section with helpful discussions of the problematic issues of canonicity and historicity. The commentary section proper is more balanced than some of the others (for instance, Myers on Chronicles) in the series. MS**

Murphy, R. E. *Wisdom Literature: Job, Proverbs, Ruth, Canticles, Ecclesiastes, and Esther.* FOTL. Eerdmans, 1981. 185 pp.

See under Job.

Paton, L. B. *The Book of Esther.* ICC. T & T Clark, 1908. xvii/339 pp.

Paton provides a large introduction, devoting much attention to text-critical matters. He is skeptical that Esther has any historical worth. An interesting discussion, from a critical perspective, on Purim is the only valuable aspect of the commentary. S*

Job

Alden, R. L. *Job.* NAC. Broadman, 1993. 464 pp.

Alden presents a readable and insightful theological interpretation of the Book of Job. He fails, however, to recognize the central issue of the book, which is the nature and origin of wisdom. Nonetheless, much can be learned from this volume. LM***

Andersen, F. I. *Job.* TOTC. Inter-Varsity, 1976. 294 pp.

This is one of the best conservative commentaries on Job. It is limited by the length restrictions of the series, but still extremely valuable as a lay commentary. LM***

Atkinson, D. *The Message of Job: Suffering and Grace.* BST. Inter-Varsity, 1991. 188 pp.

This commentary provides a very practical approach to Job. Atkinson offers little analysis of the ancient message of the book, but he does show how one major theme connects with our world. LM***

Bergant, D. *Job, Ecclesiastes.* OTM. Michael Glazier, 1982. 295 pp.

A good popularly written and moderately critical commentary on the Book of Job. In exposition, Bergant "has decided to favor those themes, images and literary forms that cluster around the broad concept of order" (23). See also under Ecclesiastes. LM***

Clines, D. J. A. *Job 1–20.* WBC. Nelson/Paternoster, 1989. cxi/501 pp.

Clines has written a stimulating and insightful commentary on Job. It is stimulating in the sense that it will get the reader thinking about the book and its issues. It is provocatively written. It is particularly strong in literary and theological analysis. The bibliographies are incredibly good. If a library only has one commentary on Job, this volume should be it (of course, it covers only the first twenty chapters). MS*****

Driver, S. R., and G. B. Gray. *Job.* ICC. T & T Clark, 1921. lxxviii/360 pp.

This volume was begun by Driver, who, when he died in 1914, bequeathed its completion to Gray. The latter actually did most of the work. Gray indicates in the introduction that he and Driver believe that the original Job excluded, among smaller passages, Job 28 (the poem on wisdom) and the Elihu speech. Very technical, but occasionally helpful notes for the scholar. S***

Gibson, J. C. L. *Job.* DSB. Westminster, 1985. ix/284 pp.

Gibson honestly reports that, even after several decades of study, he still struggles with the meaning of the Book of Job. Although, from a critical perspective, his comments will help readers struggle through this difficult biblical book themselves. LM***

Gordis, R. *The Book of Job: Commentary, New Translation, and Special Studies.* Ktav, 1978. xxxiii/602 pp.

This commentary represents years of research preceded by numerous articles and a full-length book on Job. The author provides a detailed exegesis, textual study, and philological analysis. He also provides forty-two special studies on selected topics. While definitely within the critical tradition, he is moderate and looks at the book as a whole. MS****

Habel, N. C. *The Book of Job.* OTL. Westminster/SCM, 1985. 586 pp.

Habel has produced a major critical commentary on the Book of Job. It is a fairly well-rounded commentary, but it concentrates particularly on literary features and theology. While Habel is aware of the questions surrounding the unity of Job, he treats it as a finished whole. MS***

Hartley, J. E. *The Book of Job.* NICOT. Eerdmans, 1988. xiv/591 pp.

This is one of the most recent commentaries on Job, and it is a major contribution to the study of the book. This is because it examines all the facets of the book, not necessarily because it is terribly original. It is solidly evangelical in its approach. Very well-researched. MS***

Janzen, J. G. *Job.* Interp. John Knox, 1990. viii/273 pp.

In keeping with the parameters of the series, Janzen concentrates on theological significance and contemporary relevance. He does his job admirably, basing his work on an appraisal of such works as Pope and Gordis, but often presenting new ideas. He makes a small yet significant shift away from the question "Why do the innocent suffer?" to "Why are the righteous pious?" Very helpful and stimulating. LM****

McKenna, D. L. *Job.* CC. Word, 1986. 331 pp.

McKenna concentrates on Job's "faith-development." This is a distortion of the book, which shows Job moving away and not toward God in the dialogues. McKenna appropriately examines the book as it anticipates Jesus Christ. LM**

Murphy, R. E. *Wisdom Literature: Job, Proverbs, Ruth, Canticles, Ecclesiastes, and Esther.* FOTL. Eerdmans, 1981. 185 pp.

This is the first volume to appear in the FOTL series. Although proportionately shorter than others, it is still full of information and certainly one of the best in the series. Perhaps it is more useable than the others because it is less technical. Murphy is also a very clear writer, who is concerned about the meaning of the text. The bibliographies are great (characteristic of the series). S****

Pope, M. H. *Job.* AB. Doubleday, 1965. lxxxviii/409 pp.

As with many of the Anchor Bible commentaries, this one's strength is its philological analysis. Pope is one of the very best scholars of Northwest Semitic languages and, unlike Dahood, is a very sound practitioner of comparative Semitics. This is a solid commentary, but not brilliant like his Song of Songs commentary. MS***

Rowley, H. H. *Job.* NCB. Sheffield/Marshall Pickering, 1970. xix/281 pp.

Rowley represents the best of British critical scholarship of the past generation. He was a prolific and knowledgeable writer. He offers thorough discussion of many critical issues and argues for a composite approach to the Book of Job. MS***

Psalms

Alden, R. *Psalms.* 3 vols. Moody, 1974–76. 124 pp., 124 pp., and 112 pp.

In keeping with the series, this volume is popularly written, short, and conservative. It is informed by scholarly research. L***

Allen, L. C. *Psalms 101–150.* 2d ed. WBC. Nelson, 2002. xxiv/423 pp.

This commentary covers the last third of the Psalter. It is particularly helpful in two areas: language and structure. Allen has very good insight into how the structure of a psalm contributes to its message. While he is good at getting at the message of the psalm in its Old Testament setting, he is very slow in seeing the connection between the text and the New Testament. MS****

Anderson, A. A. *Psalms*. 2 vols. NCB. Sheffield/Marshall Pickering, 1972. 966 pp.

This is a good modern treatment of the Psalms. It is a little too brief and tied to the restrictive NCB format. The Allen and Craigie volumes are much better. M***

Briggs, C. A. *Psalms*. 2 vols. ICC. T & T Clark, 1907. cx/422 pp. and viii/572 pp.

This is a highly technical, fairly dated discussion of the Psalms. It is more interesting from the perspective of the history of interpretation than for exposition. S**

Broyles, C. *Psalms*. NIBCOT. Hendrickson/Paternoster, 1999. xvi/539 pp.

A brief but solid commentary on the Psalms. One might question, however, how Broyles puts the obvious liturgical nature of the Psalms at odds with their being an expression of individual experience. He recognizes the importance of christological interpretation but does not do much with it. LM***

Craigie, P. *Psalms 1–50*. WBC. Nelson/Paternoster, 1983. 375 pp.

This is the first of the three Psalms commentaries in the Word series. As the first in the series, this volume contains introductory material concerning authorship, use, style, and theology. Craigie's commentary is the best of the modern commentaries on the Psalms in matters of language and Old Testament background and message. He is a well-known Ugaritic specialist and is able to cut through the benefits and pitfalls of recent research into the connections between Ugaritic and biblical literature. Two weaknesses of the commentary are his poetical comments and the connections that he draws (or fails to draw) with the New Testament message. This commentary is a must-buy for a serious student of the Psalms, but it should be complemented by a commentary that is strong in its theological insight (like Kidner). MS****

Dahood, M. J. *Psalms.* 3 vols. AB. Doubleday, 1965, 1968, 1970. xlvi/329 pp., xxx/399 pp., and liv/490 pp.

Dahood is (in)famous for his use of Northwest Semitic (particularly Ugaritic) in his study of the Psalms. While there is no doubt that cognate languages have helped our understanding of the Psalms, Dahood has overused them in his commentary. There is no methodological control, and even Ugaritic scholars cannot evaluate his arguments. Nonspecialists will be at a total loss. In short, this commentary is very eccentric. S*

Eaton, J. H. *Psalms.* TBC. SCM, 1967. 317 pp.

A popular, brief commentary by one of today's leading experts on the Psalms. He assigns a large role to the Israelite king. LM****

Gerstenberger, E. S. *Psalms, Part I : With an Introduction to Cultic Poetry.* FOTL. Eerdmans, 1989. *Psalms, Part 2, and Lamentations.* FOTL. Eerdmans, 2001. xv/260 pp. and xxii/543 pp.

Excellent tool for scholars because of its scholarship and bibliographies. It is extremely doubtful that ministers or laypeople will have much use for this series. Gerstenberger's comments on Lamentations are considerably shorter. S****

Kidner, D. *Psalms 1–72.* TOTC. Inter-Varsity, 1973. *Psalms 73–150.* TOTC. Inter-Varsity, 1975. x/257 pp. and vii/235 pp.

Kidner has written two volumes on the Psalms. Unfortunately, they are very brief. This is compensated for by Kidner's ability to write concisely. Thus, in spite of its brevity, this commentary is highly recommended for its theological insight and practical bent. The discussion of the Hebrew text is minimal and is not intended to be very sophisticated. However, the introductory material, particularly the discussion of the meaning of the difficult words in the psalm titles, is very helpful. This commentary is well worth its price. LM****

Knight, G. A. F. *Psalms.* 2 vols. DSB. Westminster, 1982. 350 pp. and 384 pp.

This volume, like the others in DSB, is theologically sensitive from a Christian perspective. It is moderate in its criticism, devoting more attention to the elucidation of meaning than to other aspects of study, like poetics or the Near Eastern background. LM****

Kraus, H.-J. *Psalms 1–59.* Continental Commentary. Fortress, 1988. *Psalms 60–150.* Continental Commentary. Fortress, 1993. 559 pp. and 586 pp.

This magisterial work on the Psalms represents the erudition of one of the world's preeminent experts on the Psalms, and on the Old Testament for that matter. It is a translation of a German original, the first edition of which was published in 1961; the translation is taken from the fifth edition, published in the late 1970s. The commentary is extremely technical, especially in the introduction. A section-by-section analysis of each psalm is more accessible. Kraus is as interested in theology as he is in poetic forms and *Sitz im Leben*, but this commentary, which clearly comes from the German critical tradition, is only for the extremely serious biblical scholar. S****

Mays, J. L. *Psalms.* Interp. John Knox, 1994. xvii/457 pp.

Mays has given us an exciting new commentary that focuses on the literary expression and theological message of the Psalms. It approaches the Psalms as rich statements of faith in God. The author downplays historical and form-critical approaches. He has a good feel for the Psalms as individual compositions as well as the structure of the book as a whole. He gives more comment to psalms that have had a bigger impact on later Christian theology. LM*****

Rogerson, J. W., and J. W. McKay. *Psalms.* 3 vols. CBC. Cambridge University Press, 1977. xi/243 pp., xi/193 pp., and 234 pp.

The authors have tried to "strike a balance between the spiritual, historical, form-critical and cultic approaches." They depart from the NEB in that they believe that the titles, although added later, have something to add to our understanding of the Psalms. LM***

Tate, M. *Psalms 51–100.* Word, 1990. 579 pp.

This is the third of the Word Psalms volumes to appear, and it is a suitably excellent contribution to the strong commentaries by Allen and Craigie. The one caveat— and it is not insignificant—is that it is weakest in theology of the Psalms. So read John Calvin along with these volumes. MS****

Van Gemeren, W. *Psalms.* EBC 5. Zondervan, 1991.

This commentary is major in size and contribution and should not be overlooked because it is bound with a couple of other commentaries. Indeed, if a pastor or layperson wants just one Psalms commentary, this is it. Van Gemeren deals with all aspects of the Psalms, but concentrates on the meaning and theology of the book. LM*****

Weiser, A. *The Psalms.* OTL. Westminster/SCM, 1962. 841 pp.

While not strongly recommended for purchase, this commentary is often theologically insightful. One must be aware of the neoorthodox perspective from which the author is writing and also his belief that all of the psalms fit into an annual covenant-renewal ceremony. Weiser is correct to see a close connection between the Psalms and the covenant, but mistaken to reconstruct an annual festival with which to connect them. This theory is a definite improvement, however, over Mowinckel's enthronement festival. Weiser is a theological commentator on the Psalms. There is little help in the areas of language or structure. LM**

Wilcock, M. *The Message of Psalms 1–72*. BST. Inter-Varsity, 2001. *The Message of Psalms 73–150*. BST. Inter-Varsity, 2001. 255 pp. and 288 pp.

Short, but very well-written, this is a good "starter commentary" for those who are not overly interested in the technical issues, but who simply want a solid exposition. L****

Williams, D. M. *Psalms*. CC. 2 vols. Word, 1986, 1989. 493 pp. and 543 pp.

Williams does his scholarly homework well as he attempts to help ministers and other Christian leaders communicate the message of the Psalms in their Old Testament setting. He includes some anecdotes and interesting illustrations. LM****

Wilson, G. H. *Psalms*. Vol. 1. NIVAC. Zondervan, 2002. 1,024 pp.

Wilson's commentary is strong in all three sections of the series: original meaning, bridging contexts, and contemporary significance. I cannot agree with him about the structure of the book as a whole, which is an original contribution, but the commentary has much value, especially for ministers. LM*****

Proverbs

Aitken, K. T. *Proverbs*. DSB. Westminster, 1986. 276 pp.

The introduction to this volume is one of the more critical of the series, although the bulk of the commentary provides helpful information. Interestingly, Aitken orders the material in Proverbs 10 and afterward in a topical rather than textual format. LM***

Alden, R. *Proverbs: A Commentary on an Ancient Book of Timeless Advice.* Baker, 1983. 222 pp.

This is a devotional commentary on the book. While it does discuss various translation possibilities, it is more concerned to draw applications for today. Sometimes these applications are helpful and right; others are forced and even trite. L***

Clifford, Richard J. *Proverbs.* OTL. Westminster John Knox, 1999. xvi/286 pp.

This commentary puts more emphasis on text criticism, philology, and ancient Near Eastern background than some of the other commentaries listed here. His exposition of the meaning of the Hebrew is a little less substantial than that of other commentaries, but it is still very good. MS****

Farmer, K. A. *Proverbs and Ecclesiastes.* ITC. Handsel, 1991.

This interesting, nontechnical commentary takes a canonical approach, with substantial discussion of the theology of the book and its significance for contemporary society. LM***

Fox, Michael V. *Proverbs 1–9.* AB. Doubleday, 2000. xix/474 pp.

This is an excellent commentary both because the series allows more space than other commentaries and because Fox is a master interpreter. The only drawback is that it covers just the first nine chapters. Hopefully, we will not have to wait too long for the rest of the commentary to appear. MS*****

Garrett, D. A. *Proverbs. Ecclesiastes. Song of Songs.* NAC. Broadman, 1993. 448 pp. (252 pp. devoted to Proverbs).

Garrett's introduction is an interesting and helpful conservative approach to the issues of historical and literary structure. His comments on the text itself are helpful, but too brief. LM***

Hubbard, D. A. *Proverbs.* CC. Word, 1989. 487 pp.

While somewhat more scholarly in tone than other commentaries in the series, Hubbard's contribution is still quite readable and achieves the purposes of CC. The introduction, before beginning the commentary proper, highlights six principles of interpretation. Hubbard gives important guidelines to properly understanding the book's forms of speech and literary devices. The section on Proverbs 10ff. orders the discussion by topic rather than verse by verse. LM****

Kidner, D. *Proverbs.* TOTC. Inter-Varsity, 1964. 192 pp.

This small commentary is packed with helpful insight and comments on the text. It is exegetically sensitive, theologically helpful, and orthodox. However, for serious study of Proverbs it should be supplemented by a fuller commentary like McKane's. LM****

McKane, W. *Proverbs: A New Approach.* OTL. Westminster/SCM, 1970. xvii/670 pp.

This commentary is a significant contribution to the study of Proverbs, even if the critical conclusions are difficult to appreciate. McKane differentiates the instruction genre of 1–9, 22:17–24:22, 31:1–9 from the sentence literature of 10–22:16, 24:23–34, and 25–29. However, this commentary is invaluable for the study of the language of Proverbs. The way to use it is to turn to McKane's translation on pages 211–61, where he references his discussion of individual verses. A further debatable conclusion of his study is his division of the sentence literature into three classes. A must for scholarly enquiry into Proverbs, but of doubtful value to the layperson or pastor. MS****

Murphy, R. E. *Wisdom Literature: Job, Proverbs, Ruth, Canticles, Ecclesiastes, and Esther.* FOTL. Eerdmans, 1981. 185 pp.

See under Job.

Murphy, R. E. *Proverbs.* WBC. Nelson/Paternoster, 1998. lxxiv/306 pp.

Murphy is a preeminent interpreter of wisdom literature. MS★★★★

Murphy, R. E., and E. Huwiler. *Proverbs, Ecclesiastes, Song of Songs.* NIBCOT. Hendrickson/Paternoster, 1999. xvi/ 312 pp.

Murphy, an acknowledged master of the subject, wrote the section on Proverbs, but if one is really interested in his opinions, it is better to get his fuller treatment in the Word series. Perhaps laypeople might find this a more accessible version. LM★★

Perdue, Leo G. *Proverbs.* Interp. John Knox, 2000. xi/289 pp.

This commentary focuses on the literary, structural, ethical, and theological issues of the Book of Proverbs. Its perspective is critical but moderately applied; a source of many good insights. LM★★★★

Ross, A. *Proverbs.* EBC 5. Zondervan, 1991.

This commentary is a bonus in the volume featuring Van Gemeren's commentary on the Psalms. It is well worth adding to your library. LM★★★

Scott, R. B. Y. *Proverbs, Ecclesiastes.* AB. Doubleday, 1965. liii/257 pp.

This is not one of the better commentaries in the Anchor Bible series. It represents a classically critical approach to Proverbs. It is not particularly strong in any area of research. S★

Toy, C. H. *Proverbs.* ICC. T & T Clark, 1899. xxxvi/554 pp.

Toy was one of the leading scholars of the turn of the nineteenth century, but his commentary is now dated in its critical methodology and conclusions. S★★

van Leeuwen, Raymond. "Proverbs." In *The New Interpreter's Bible.* Abingdon, 1997. 5:19–264.

This commentary exposits the text and also reflects on it theologically. Written from a progressive evangelical perspective, it is one of the best commentaries on Proverbs. LM*****

Whybray, R. N. *The Book of Proverbs.* CBC. Cambridge University Press, 1972. x/197 pp.

A good, competent study of the book from a critical perspective. Whybray distinguishes secular from religious proverbs. He studies the book in its ancient Near Eastern setting. LM**

Ecclesiastes

Barton, G. A. *Ecclesiastes.* ICC. T & T Clark, 1908. xiv/212 pp.

Barton is a good example of a turn-of-the-century critical scholar. This commentary is very detailed and certainly not for the nonscholar. Barton has thorough text-critical discussions and tries to argue a close connection between Ecclesiastes and Greek thought. S*

Bergant, D. *Job, Ecclesiastes.* OTM. Michael Glazier, 1982. 295 pp.

See under Job.

Brown, W. *Ecclesiastes.* Interp. John Knox, 2000. xiv/143 pp.

Explores the connections between Ecclesiastes and the ancient tale of Gilgamesh as both examine the significance of life. He believes that the Teacher "offers modern readers the dread and delight of the everyday, the glory of the ordinary." Worth reading. LM***

Crenshaw, J. L. *Ecclesiastes.* OTL. Westminster/SCM, 1987. 192 pp.

Crenshaw's approach may be described as moderately critical. However, this is an excellent commentary. It is not too technical (one gets the feeling that Crenshaw is holding himself back), but it is a profound approach to the book. Highly recommended. MS****

Davidson, R. *Ecclesiastes and Song of Solomon.* DSB. Westminster, 1986. 168 pp.

This volume is one of the more critical of the series, especially on such issues as the date and composition of Ecclesiastes. Nonetheless, it provides a helpful and non-dogmatic perspective. LM***

Eaton, Michael A. *Ecclesiastes.* TOTC. Inter-Varsity, 1983. 159 pp.

Eaton writes well, with a nontechnical audience in mind. He has many good insights into the text, but the commentary is marred by his view that the orthodoxy of Ecclesiastes can be preserved only by turning Qohelet into a "preacher of joy"—quite an exegetical trick. LM**

Farmer, K. A. *Proverbs and Ecclesiastes: Who Knows What Is Good?* ITC. Handsel, 1991.

Farmer notes the widely divergent interpretive approaches to this book and considers it a type of deliberate ambiguity. She notes that the key Hebrew term *hebel* has been translated as denoting either meaninglessness or transience. She advocates a reading that allows the reader to "Decide for Yourself!" (146). There is much of value in this commentary, but its suspension of judgment is unsatisfying and unnecessary. LM***

Fox, M. V. *Qohelet and His Contradictions.* Almond, 1989. 384 pp. [Reissued in a new edition as *A Rereading of Ecclesiastes: A Time to Tear Down and a Time to Build Up.* Eerdmans, 1999. xvii/422 pp.]

This book may be divided into two parts. The first half treats the book as a whole and offers some tantalizing essays on some key themes, arguing for instance that the key phrase of the book is not "vanity" or "meaninglessness" but rather "absurdity." The second part of the book is a commentary with an emphasis on philology, textual criticism, the book's structure, and interpretation. Fox's idea of Ecclesiastes as a framed monologue is very provocative. MS****

Garrett, D. A. *Proverbs. Ecclesiastes. Song of Songs.* NAC. Broadman, 1993. 447 pp. (93 pp. devoted to Ecclesiastes).

See also under Proverbs and Song of Songs. Garrett proposes that the main purpose of the Book of Ecclesiastes is to impress upon its readers that they are moral. He devotes considerable effort to criticizing rival views. The commentary itself is quite short. LM**

Ginsburg, C. D. *The Song of Songs and Coheleth.* 1857; Ktav, 1970. xliv/528 pp.

Ginsburg was an extremely learned scholar who was well-versed in both Christian and Jewish scholarship. His approach is dated, but the prolegomenon, written by S. Blank, attempts to bring certain discussions up to date. S***

Hubbard, D. A. *Beyond Futility.* Eerdmans, 1976. 128 pp.

This short, lay-oriented commentary is extremely insightful, particularly in its comments on how Christ moves beyond the futility of Qohelet. LM****

Kaiser, W. C., Jr. *Ecclesiastes: Total Life.* Moody, 1979. 128 pp.

Kaiser has written a very readable commentary on the Book of Ecclesiastes. Unfortunately, he takes an untenable approach to the book, turning the main speaker Qohelet into an orthodox "preacher of joy." LM**

Kidner, D. *The Message of Ecclesiastes: A Time to Mourn and a Time to Dance.* Inter-Varsity, 1976. 110 pp.

This commentary is very popular and may be the best on the Book of Ecclesiastes. It is well-written and sensible in its approach to Ecclesiastes. Shows application to life as well. LM****

Longman, T., III. *Ecclesiastes.* NICOT. Eerdmans, 1998. xvi/306 pp.

This commentary deals with the philology (providing a new translation), the literary character, and theological message of the book. Longman argues that the author is not Solomon, but that Ecclesiastes adopts a Solomonic persona to show the meaninglessness of life. Takes a canonical-christocentric approach to the meaning of the book.

Murphy, R. E. *Ecclesiastes.* WBC. Nelson/Paternoster, 1992. 254 pp.

Murphy is one of the preeminent interpreters of wisdom, and serious students of Ecclesiastes will read this commentary carefully. He is particularly interesting to read for his translation and exegetical notes. However, there are better commentaries to get at the original meaning and theological significance of Ecclesiastes. MS★★★★

Murphy, R. E. *Wisdom Literature: Job, Proverbs, Ruth, Canticles, Ecclesiastes, and Esther.* FOTL. Eerdmans, 1981. 185 pp.

See under Job.

Murphy, R. E., and E. Huwiler. *Proverbs, Ecclesiastes, Song of Songs.* NIBCOT. Hendrickson/Paternoster, 1999. 312 pp.

Huwiler produced the interpretation of Ecclesiastes here. She makes a fundamental error in not differentiating the theology of Qohelet from that of the book as a whole. She basically sees the book as affirming the struggle of postmodernism. LM★★

Provan, I. *Ecclesiastes/Song of Songs.* NIVAC. Zondervan/Hodder & Stoughton, 2001. 399 pp.

Provan has written one of the most interesting commentaries on these two intriguing books. Even though one may not agree with his final conclusions, his thinking is provocative and will lead the reader to think through old issues. One example is his understanding of the Song as a drama having three main characters. The basic plot as he reconstructs it is that Solomon has forced a country girl into his harem, though she continues to love the shepherd boy back home. The theme of the book proclaims that true love resists coerced legal love. LM****

Scott, R. B. Y. *Proverbs, Ecclesiastes.* AB. Doubleday, 1965. xii/257 pp.

See under Proverbs. Ecclesiastes is treated very briefly, almost like an afterthought. S*

Seow, C.-L. *Ecclesiastes.* AB. Doubleday, 1997. xxiv/419 pp.

This readable yet scholarly commentary argues for a specific date of the book in the Persian period. While this argument is not compelling, the theological notes are often insightful. MS****

Whybray, R. N. *Ecclesiastes.* NCB. Sheffield/Marshall Pickering, 1989. xxiii/179 pp.

Whybray, a prolific and respected English Old Testament scholar, has written on Ecclesiastes before, most notably in his article "Qohelet: Preacher of Joy" (*JSOT* 23 [1982]: 87–98). Here, as there, he leans toward an interpretation that sees Qohelet as a realist who, in spite of clearly seeing all the problems of a world living under the effects of the curse, nonetheless believes that God wants people to enjoy life. Whybray argues that Ecclesiastes is late (third century B.C.) and under some Greek influence. MS****

Wright, J. S. *Ecclesiastes.* EBC 5. Zondervan, 1991.

Even though John Walton makes an admirable effort to salvage this commentary by adding notes, the section on Ecclesiastes is not worth the money alone. However, it is bound with Van Gemeren's Psalms commentary; thus, you should buy the volume but not expect much from Wright's contribution. LM*

Song of Songs

Carr, G. L. *Song of Songs.* TOTC. Inter-Varsity, 1984. 175 pp.

This is a good popular exposition of the Song. Much scholarly research stands behind it. Carr takes a flexible approach to authorship and makes an adequate presentation of alternative approaches to the book. He himself advocates a "natural reading." LM***

Davidson, R. *Ecclesiastes and Song of Solomon.* DSB. Westminster, 1986. viii/162 pp.

See also under Ecclesiastes. Davidson rightly takes the view that the Song is a collection of love poems. He gives a helpful analysis of the imagery of the book. LM****

Garrett, D. A. *Proverbs. Ecclesiastes. Song of Songs.* NAC. Broadman, 1993. 447 pp. (85 pp. devoted to the Song of Songs).

See also under Proverbs and Ecclesiastes. Garrett advocates the Solomonic authorship of the book. He treats the Song as a unified love poem and writes that it is neither an allegory nor a drama. LM**

Gledhill, T. *The Message of the Song of Songs: The Lyrics of Love.* Inter-Varsity, 1994. 254 pp.

This is a model popular commentary. It is well-written, easy to read, yet profound. Also, Gledhill has an excellent literary sense; he neither simply adopts traditional readings nor gives in to the excesses of contemporary psychological readings of the text. LM*****

Keel, O. *The Song of Songs.* Continental Commentary. Fortress, 1994. ix/308 pp.

Keel demonstrates excellent literary and overall exegetical sensibilities. He even makes some insightful theological comments. The translation/writing is excellent, even humorous at times. A special feature, not unusual to Keel's work, is the presence of copies of relevant Near Eastern art. SM*****

Knight, G. A. F., and F. W. Golka. *The Song of Songs and*

Jonah: Revelation of God. ITC. Handsel, 1988. ix/136 pp.

Knight's contribution is an interesting reassertion of the divine-human aspects of the relationship depicted in the Song of Songs. LM***

Longman, Tremper, III. *Song of Songs.* NICOT. Eerdmans, 2001. xvi/238 pp.

My commentary on the Song has a relatively lengthy introduction discussing such pivotal interpretive issues as genre and ancient Near Eastern background as well as the controversial subject of authorship. The Song is understood to be an anthology of twenty-three love poems. The theological significance of the book is fully discussed. ML

Murphy, R. E. *Wisdom Literature: Job, Proverbs, Ruth, Canticles, Ecclesiastes, and Esther.* FOTL. Eerdmans, 1981. 185 pp.

See under Job.

Murphy, R. E. *The Song of Songs.* Hermeneia. Fortress/ SCM, 1990. xxii/227 pp.

Murphy provides an excellent critical reading of the text. He emphasizes its final form and is concerned with theological issues. His lengthy introduction gives a helpful survey of the history of interpretation, issues of prosody, and basic interpretive approach. MS****

Murphy, R. E., and E. Huwiler. *Proverbs, Ecclesiastes, Song of Songs.* NIBCOT. Hendrickson/Paternoster, 1999. 312 pp.

See also under Proverbs and Ecclesiastes. Huwiler's analysis of the Song of Songs is much better than her treatment of Ecclesiastes. LM***

Pope, M. H. *Song of Songs.* AB. Doubleday, 1977. xxi/743 pp.

This is one of the best commentaries written on any

book of the Bible. It contains a wealth of linguistic, literary, and historical information. The history of interpretation, comparative sections, and fifty-five-page bibliography are worth the price of the book. Pope fairly represents positions different from his own. His overall approach to the book as connected with the love and death cults of the ancient world leaves much to be desired, but is interesting. MS*****

Provan, I. *Ecclesiastes/Song of Songs.* NIVAC. Zondervan/Hodder & Stoughton, 2001. 399 pp.

See under Ecclesiastes.

Snaith, J. G. *Song of Songs.* NCB. Sheffield/Marshall Pickering, 1993. 140 pp.

Insights to be found here and there, but really too brief to compete with the other commentaries available. LM**

Isaiah

Baltzer, K. *Deutero-Isaiah: A Commentary on Isaiah 40–55.* Hermeneia. Fortress, 2001. 400 pp.

Baltzer treats Deutero-Isaiah as a six-act liturgical drama that was performed during Passover/Mazzot. Hymns mark the end of acts. He dates this material later than even traditional historical criticism (450–400 B.C.). Scholars will need to consult this commentary. S****

Blenkinsopp, J. *Isaiah 1–39.* AB. Doubleday, 2000. *Isaiah 40–55.* Doubleday, 2002. xix/525 pp. and xvii/411pp.

Blenkinsopp takes a synchronic and diachronic approach to the book, but it is hard to see the former for the latter. Though contrary to the current trend that it is virtually impossible to get to authentic eighth-century Isaiah, even in chapters 1–39, he does hold that there is a substratum of such material, though he believes "the eighth-century B.C.E. prophet has been buried under an exegetical mountain" (*Isaiah 1–39*, 90). Both volumes have lengthy and informative introductions as well as extensive bibliographies. S****

Childs, B. S. *Isaiah*. OTL. Westminster John Knox, 2001. xx/555 pp.

Well worth it to get Childs's canon-conscious take on the book. Not quite as well-done in depth and detail as the much earlier Exodus commentary, but helpful to see how he manages what he considers to be the compositional history of the book with the final form's theological message. MS***

Clements, R. E. *Isaiah 1–39*. NCB. Sheffield, 1980. xvi/301 pp.

Clements is an evangelical who practices a moderate higher criticism. He is one of the most prolific British writers in the field of Old Testament. He has a good writing style and practices sensitive exegesis. However, his critical perspective mars many of his insights. MS***

Goldingay, J. *Isaiah*. NIBCOT. Hendrickson/Paternoster, 2001. x/397 pp.

Goldingay presents a very readable and insightful interpretation of Isaiah in a compact format. Some readers will not like his approach to the history of the book's composition, which he attributes not only to the prophet (whom he calls the Ambassador), but to others whom he terms the Disciple, the Poet, and the Preacher. It would be a great mistake for people put off by these conclusions to ignore this important commentary. Only its length keeps it from being a five-star commentary. MS****

Gray, G. B. *Isaiah 1–27*. ICC. T & T Clark, 1912. ci/472 pp.

This is a detailed and scholarly presentation of turn-of-the-century critical thought on the Book of Isaiah. S**

Grogan, G. W. *Isaiah*. EBC 6. Zondervan, 1986.

Grogan gives a fine theological exposition of Isaiah from a conservative historical perspective. LM****

Hanson, P. D. *Isaiah 40–66.* Interp. John Knox, 1995. 255 pp.

Hanson's volume complements Seitz's commentary (listed below) by treating "Second" Isaiah. Like Seitz, Hanson takes a moderately critical stance, arguing that, though there are many literary and theological connections throughout the book as a whole, these chapters come from a hand other than the eighth-century prophet. It is a work from the exilic and early exilic periods. Though this historical conclusion will disappoint more conservative readers, it should not keep them from appreciating the fine theological analysis of the book. M****

Herbert, A. S. *The Book of the Prophet Isaiah.* 2 vols. CBC. Cambridge University Press, 1975. x/219 pp. and ix/204 pp.

Herbert gives considerable attention to the historical background and the phenomenology of prophecy. LM**

Kaiser, O. *Isaiah 1–39.* 2 vols. OTL. Westminster/SCM, 1972. xx/170 pp. and xix/412 pp.

Kaiser represents the best of German critical scholarship on the Book of Isaiah. S***

Knight, G. A. F. *Isaiah 40–55: Servant Theology.* ITC. Handsel, 1984. *Isaiah 55–66: The New Israel.* ITC. Handsel, 1985. ix/204 pp. and xvii/126 pp.

Although he argues against an eighth-century date for the prophecy, Knight brackets historical-critical concerns. He shows great sensitivity to exegetical and theological issues. LM***

McKenzie, J. L. *Second Isaiah.* AB. Doubleday, 1968. lxxi/225 pp.

Although its title might lead the reader to think otherwise, McKenzie actually comments on both what he calls Second Isaiah and Third Isaiah. The latter he thinks is made up of miscellaneous oracles from anonymous sources. There are better commentaries on the subject, in both the critical and evangelical camps. S**

Motyer, J. Alec. *The Prophecy of Isaiah: An Introduction and Commentary.* Inter-Varsity, 1994. 544 pp.

This commentary represents three decades of work by the author on the biblical book. It is thoroughly researched and thought-out. It represents the best of a conservative evangelical approach to the book at the end of the twentieth century. It is best in matters theological. MS****

Motyer, J. Alec. *Isaiah.* TOTC. Inter-Varsity, 1999. 408 pp.

Motyer has also written a longer and more technical commentary also referred to in this guide. Though the approach to the book is substantially the same, the present volume is more accessible to laypeople. Motyer and Oswalt provide the most lucid exposition of Isaiah from a traditional viewpoint that sees the whole book as coming largely from the eighth century. ML****

North, C. R. *Isaiah 40–55.* TBC. SCM, 1952. 158 pp.

North was one of the greatest critical interpreters of Isaiah of the past generation with a particular interest in the Servant Songs. He brings incredible expertise to this popular commentary. His approach to the Servant Songs is particularly interesting and noteworthy. M****

Oswalt, J. *Isaiah 1–39.* NICOT. Eerdmans, 1986. *Isaiah 40–66.* NICOT. Eerdmans, 1998. xiii/746 pp. and xviii/755 pp.

These volumes are solidly conservative and well-researched. MS****

Ridderbos, J. *Isaiah.* BSC. Zondervan, 1985. 580 pp.

This commentary is a translation of a Dutch original first published in 1950/51. It is oriented toward the minister. Ridderbos is a top-flight scholar. He accepts the essential unity of Isaiah, although admitting some secondary glosses added by Isaiah's disciples. The commentary has the advantages and disadvantages of a one-volume commentary on such a long and complex biblical book. It is easy to digest, but often superficial (largely due to length constraints). It is written from a Reformed, conservative perspective. MS***

Sawyer, J. F. A. *Isaiah.* 2 vols. DSB. Westminster, 1984, 1986. 280 pp.

Sawyer accepts the common critical understanding of Isaiah as having been composed by different individuals inspired by the original eighth-century prophet. In the commentary proper, however, he does not deal with such historical issues; rather, he concentrates on the meaning of the text for today. LM***

Seitz, C. R. *Isaiah 1–39.* Interp. John Knox, 1993. xvi/271 pp.

This very readable commentary presents the best moderately critical approach to the Book of Isaiah. Literary context takes the fore in Seitz's interpretation of Isaiah's oracles. He does not bypass the historical setting though it is here that evangelicals will have the most difficulty. MS****

Sweeney, M. A. *Isaiah 1–39 with an Introduction to Prophetic Literature.* FOTL. Eerdmans, 1996. xix/547 pp.

For those who want an up-to-date, learned, and well-written introduction to the form criticism of Isaiah this is the best source. In keeping with the series, the issues and discussion are too technical for lay readers, and conservative readers will not like some of his conclusions, but this is an excellent piece of work. MS*****

Watts, J. D. W. *Isaiah.* 2 vols. WBC. Nelson/Paternoster, 1985, 1987. lvii/449 pp. and xxiii/385 pp.

Watts has written a commentary on the canonical form

of the book. He is not concerned with prehistory, but interprets the book in its present form. This form points to a fifth-century date for the book, although the author used materials from earlier (eighth-century) settings. Watts proposes a twelvefold structure to the book (in two [chaps. 1–39; 40–66] parts) that follows a kind of chronological flow. (Reviewers question his approach here.) This is an interesting and provocative commentary. MS***

Westermann, C. *Isaiah 40–66*. OTL. Westminster/SCM, 1969. iv/429 pp.

This volume completes Kaiser's first two volumes in the OTL series. Westermann here offers a commentary on what he calls Deutero- and Trito-Isaiah. Westermann is always insightful, and this commentary should not be ignored because of its critical basis. MS****

Whybray, R. N. *Isaiah 40–66*. NCB. Sheffield/Marshall Pickering, 1980. 301 pp.

Whybray divides his commentary between chapters 40–55 (Deutero-Isaiah) and 56–66 (Trito-Isaiah). He carefully describes the historical background of Deutero-Isaiah in the neo-Babylonian period. He applies the form-critical method to the elucidation of the text. His exposition is clear and scholarly, which is what we expect from Whybray. The format of the series, however, is very restricting. LM***

Widyapranawa, S. H. *Isaiah 1–39: The Lord Is Our Savior.* ITC. Handsel, 1990. xiv/266 pp.

This commentary is produced by an Old Testament professor from Indonesia with the hope that he might set the teaching of the prophet within a third-world perspective. While he does a competent job of interpretation, there is not much practical application to contemporary society. The introduction is virtually nonexistent. LM***

Wildberger, H. *Isaiah 1–12.* Continental Commentary.

Fortress, 1991. *Isaiah 13–27.* Continental Commentary. Fortress, 1997. *Isaiah 28–39.* Continental Commentary. Fortress, 2002. x/524 pp., x/624 pp., 720 pp.

This detailed, close reading of the Book of Isaiah covers most of the main avenues of research into a biblical book: text, source, form, theology, and so forth. It is from a critical approach. The bibliographies are extensive. S****

Young, E. J. *The Book of Isaiah.* 3 vols. Eerdmans, 1965, 1969, 1972. xii/534 pp., 604 pp., and 579 pp.

Young's commentary was originally in the NICOT series, but the series floundered after his work came out and has only been revived in the past decade (without Young's commentary; see Oswalt). Young was a meticulous and detailed scholar, which is evident in his work here. He is a better philologist than literary scholar or biblical theologian, but the commentary is well worth the money. The commentary takes a very conservative approach to Isaiah. Young's writing style is tedious. MS**

Jeremiah

Boadt, L. *Jeremiah 1–25.* OTM. Michael Glazier, 1982. *Jeremiah 26–52, Habakkuk, Zephaniah, Nahum.* OTM. Michael Glazier, 1982. xxviii/213 pp. and xii/276 pp.

A popular two-volume theological commentary on four prophets from the latter half of the seventh century. Boadt treats them together because they offer different perspectives on the same historical events. LM***

Bright, J. *Jeremiah.* AB. Doubleday, 1965. cxliv/372 pp.

This is one of the better commentaries on Jeremiah, although it is written from a moderately critical angle. Bright has good theological and literary sense. One disconcerting feature of this commentary is its arrangement. Bright has chosen to depart from Jeremiah's more topical arrangement and has commented on the text in a reconstructed chronological order. MS***

Brueggemann, W. *Jeremiah 1–25: To Pluck Up, to Tear Down.* ITC. Handsel, 1988. *Jeremiah 26–52: To Build, to Plant.* ITC. Handsel, 1991. x/289 pp. and xi/298 pp. [Also available as *A Commentary on Jeremiah: Exile and Homecoming.* Eerdmans, 1998. xiv/502 pp.]

Brueggemann provides an easy-to-read and contemporary interpretation of the Book of Jeremiah. As usual, he is thought-provoking in his reading. LM★★★★

Carroll, R. P. *The Book of Jeremiah.* OTL. Westminster/ SCM, 1986. 874 pp.

Carroll includes an excellent bibliography. His commentary emphasizes a redaction-critical approach to the book in an attempt to reconcile what he calls the "disparate *personae* of Jeremiah represented by the various levels of tradition in it" (37). S★★★

Clements, R. E. *Jeremiah.* Interp. John Knox, 1988. xi/276 pp.

Clements adopts a moderately critical approach to questions of composition and authorship. He concentrates on integrating historical background and theological message. The book is clearly written and profitable. LM★★★

Craigie, P. C., P. H. Kelley, and J. F. Drinkard, Jr. *Jeremiah 1–25.* WBC. Nelson/Paternoster, 1991. xlvii/389 pp.

Craigie died in a car accident after finishing only the first seven chapters in this commentary. Kelley and Drinkard combined to finish this volume; G. Keown is the announced author of the second volume on Jeremiah. The volume as a whole is consistent with Craigie's high level of scholarship. The volume is especially helpful in matters of language and form. The analysis of content is a little thin, and theological reflection is at a minimum. The volume's bibliographies are extensive. MS★★★★

Cunliffe-Jones, H. *Jeremiah.* TBC. Macmillan, 1961.

The author builds on a moderately critical approach to

the text in order to emphasize Jeremiah's theology and the relevance of the book for today. He also focuses on Jeremiah's personality as it is disclosed in the text. LM***

Davidson, R. *Jeremiah and Lamentations.* 2 vols. DSB. Westminster, 1983, 1985.

Davidson devotes all of the first volume and most of the second to a study of the prophecy of Jeremiah. While he accepts a moderately critical approach to the text, he does not present critical discussions in the commentary. The result is a popularly written and helpful exposition. LM****

Dearman, J. A. *Jeremiah/Lamentations.* NIVAC. Zondervan/Hodder & Stoughton, 2002. 488 pp.

A very sensitive theological reading that also brings these two books into touch with the contemporary world. In keeping with the series, Dearman does not deal with technical issues. LM*****

Guest, J. *Jeremiah, Lamentations.* CC. Word, 1988. 390 pp.

Guest writes with a good understanding of the book in its Old Testament background and awareness of its New Testament connections. His writing style is engaging, and he provides insightful comment. LM***

Harrison, R. K. *Jeremiah and Lamentations.* TOTC. Inter-Varsity, 1973. 240 pp.

Due to its size restrictions, this commentary is unable to compare with some of the others as a major research tool. However, it is an excellent commentary for laypeople. The emphasis is on history, philology, and theology. LM***

Holladay, W. L. *Jeremiah.* 2 vols. Hermeneia. Fortress/ SCM, 1986, 1989. xxii/682 pp. and xxxi/543 pp.

This is a major contribution to Jeremiah studies written from a form-critical perspective; it should be consulted

by everyone who does serious work on the book. Like
the others in the series, it is a well-presented commentary. MS****

Huey, F. B., Jr. *Jeremiah. Lamentations*. NAC. Broadman,
1993. 512 pp.

This commentary, in keeping with the series, emphasizes the theological message of the book in its historical context. What it says is true and helpful, as far as it
goes, and that is its main shortcoming. It is rather thin.
Professor Huey represents a traditional conservative approach to the books that he studies. LM**

Jones, D. R. *Jeremiah*. NCB. Sheffield/Marshall Pickering,
1992. 557 pp.

This commentary produced by a competent senior scholar
has a higher level of confidence in the history of the
book than most critics. He gives a strong synchronic exposition, but, due to the constraints of the series, the
analysis is not detailed. LM***

Keown, G. L., P. J. Scalise, and T. G. Smothers. *Jeremiah
26–52*. WBC. Nelson/Paternoster, 1995.

When the original contributor to the Word series on Jeremiah, Peter Craigie, died, it was an odd decision to assign the rest of the book to four other scholars (including
Allen in vol. 1). MS***

Lundbom, J. R. *Jeremiah 1–20*. AB. Doubleday, 1999. 934
pp.

This is a brilliant commentary on the book in its original meaning, though Lundbom is not interested in Jeremiah's theology. A must-buy for those ministers and
scholars who are really interested in looking at the book.
MS*****

McKane, W. *A Critical and Exegetical Commentary on Jeremiah*. 2 vols. ICC. T & T Clark, 1986, 1996. cxxii/658
pp. and clxxiv/785 pp.

This is an example of the "new generation" ICC commentaries. Not many Old Testament commentaries are out yet. The new commentaries have the same critical concerns as the older series: textual criticism, philology, and historical matters. There is little theological reflection. However, since the newer volumes take into account recent advances in scholarship, these volumes are more valuable than the older ones. McKane's volumes have extensive text-critical and redaction-critical discussions. A must for all scholars, but just as well ignored by most laypersons and ministers. S***

Nicholson, E. W. *Jeremiah.* 2 vols. CBC. Cambridge University Press, 1973–75. xii/220 pp. and xi/247 pp.

The introduction helpfully reconstructs the historical background to the prophecy. Nicholson examines the literary growth of the book from Jeremiah the prophet through the Deuteronomic school. LM**

Thompson, J. A. *The Book of Jeremiah.* NICOT. Eerdmans, 1979. xii/819 pp.

Thompson takes a more traditional and evangelical approach to the book. However, he does allow for some non-Jeremiah parts. He treats Jeremiah as a real person in a definite historical setting. Well worth getting. MS****

Lamentations

Berlin, A. *Lamentations: A Commentary.* OTL. Westminster John Knox, 2002. xxvi/135 pp.

Berlin devotes a large part of this relatively short commentary to the introduction. Though short, her work contains much substance and insight. She focuses on literary features, particularly the book's metaphors, to get at the theology of the book. She lists "purity, mourning, repentance, and the Davidic covenant" as particularly important themes in the book (ix). She has an admirable agnosticism concerning historical-critical issues and studies the book in relation to the background of other ancient Near Eastern literature. MS*****

Davidson, R. *Jeremiah and Lamentations.* Vol. 2. DSB. Westminster, 1985. 228 pp.

See also under Jeremiah. Davidson's comments on Lamentations are vivid and concise. He uses a number of modern analogies to bring the horror of the destruction of Jerusalem to life. LM****

Dearman, J. A. *Jeremiah/Lamentations.* NIVAC. Zondervan/Hodder & Stoughton, 2002. 488 pp.

See under Jeremiah.

Dobbs-Allsopp, F. W. *Lamentations.* Interp. John Knox, 2002. xiv/159 pp.

Dobbs-Allsopp gives a very sensitive theological and existential interpretation to the book. This commentary is especially helpful to those who preach and want to bridge from Lamentations to the contemporary situation. LM*****

Gerstenberger, E. *Psalms, Part 2, and Lamentations.* FOTL. Eerdmans, 2001. xxii/543 pp.

See under Psalms.

Harrison, R. K. *Jeremiah and Lamentations.* TOTC. InterVarsity, 1973. 240 pp.

See under Jeremiah.

Hillers, D. R. *Lamentations.* 2d ed. AB. Doubleday, 1992. xiv/175 pp.

A good commentary. It does a good job elucidating the book's Near Eastern literary background. MS***

Huey, F. B., Jr. *Jeremiah. Lamentations.* NAC. Broadman, 1993. 512 pp.

See under Jeremiah.

Martin-Achard, R., and S. Paul Re'emi. *Amos and Lamen-*

tations: God's People in Crisis. ITC. Handsel, 1984. viii/ 134 pp.

Re'emi gives a balanced, commonsense interpretation of Lamentations. See also under Amos. LM***

Provan, I. *Lamentations.* NCB. Sheffield/Marshall Pickering, 1991. 134 pp.

Very clearly written and cogent discussions of the book's difficulties, though I think he may be a bit overly skeptical in pinning down the book's historical setting. Understands the book to be "man's struggle to speak in the face of God's silence." LM*****

Ezekiel

Allen, L. C. *Ezekiel 1–19.* WBC. Nelson/Paternoster, 1994. *Ezekiel 20–48.* WBC. Nelson/Paternoster, 1990. 342 pp. and xxviii/301 pp.

Brownlee's death interrupted the completion of his commentary on Ezekiel. Allen now has completed his work. Brownlee's approach was somewhat eccentric, and Allen departs from it and goes his own way. While this divergence is unfortunate, it may be the best for the series. Allen is concerned with both the final form of the book as well as its composition. In this regard, he sees himself mediating the positions represented by Greenberg and Zimmerli. MS****

Blenkinsopp, J. *Ezekiel.* Interp. John Knox, 1990. vi/242 pp.

This series, written from a moderately critical perspective, is a delight to read. It is rich in theological insight and very accessible. Blenkinsopp's commentary is no exception. In the introduction, he clearly explains his view of how a prophetic book grows and applies it to Ezekiel. He focuses on religious and theological issues, with a special concentration on the presence/absence of God. LM****

Block, D. I. *The Book of Ezekiel 1–24.* NICOT. Eerdmans,

1997. *The Book of Ezekiel 25–48.* NICOT. Eerdmans, 1998. xxi/887 pp. and xxiii/826 pp.

Every serious student of Ezekiel needs to have this commentary in their library. Block writes very clearly and exposits this very difficult prophecy in an accessible manner. It is long, but he uses the pages to good purpose. He interacts with other commentaries without making it too tedious. MS*****

Brownlee, W. H. *Ezekiel 1–19.* WBC. Nelson/Paternoster, 1986. xlii/320 pp.

Brownlee had a high view of Scripture, but this did not prevent him from seeing considerable editorial activity and redaction over a long period of time, resulting in the book that we have before us. Yet "despite all this editorial activity, the major contents of the book of Ezekiel are genuine, and whatever editing they later received serves to emphasize the prophet's greatness" (xl). MS***

Carley, K. W. *The Book of the Prophet Ezekiel.* CBC. Cambridge University Press, 1974. 331 pp.

Carley writes clearly and has produced a competent, critical commentary for the layperson. LM***

Cooke, G. A. *Ezekiel.* ICC. T & T Clark, 1936. xlvii/541 pp.

This volume is less tedious than most in the series. Cooke is both scholarly and thorough. His approach is critical, but tinged with piety. The survey of the historical background is comprehensive but dated. S***

Cooper, L. E., Sr. *Ezekiel.* NAC. Broadman, 1994. 440 pp.

This commentary is informative on a basic level, but not too profound or thought-provoking. It adopts a dispensationalist and premillennial approach, which I personally find difficult to accept. So if that is your view, add a star. LM**

Craigie, P. C. *Ezekiel.* DSB. Westminster, 1983. x/321 pp.

Craigie's brief yet helpful commentary is extremely readable. It opens up this difficult book for the interested lay reader. It takes an evangelical approach to the book. LM★★★★

Duguid, I. *Ezekiel*. NIVAC. Zondervan/Hodder & Stoughton, 1999. 568 pp.

Duguid's volume is an excellent example of the strengths of the NIVAC series. He is known in the scholarly world as a leading analyst of the prophet, but he has also served as a minister, and his pastoral sensitivities come through in this accessible commentary on an often enigmatic prophet. LM★★★★★

Eichrodt, W. *Ezekiel*. OTL. Westminster/SCM, 1970. xiv/594 pp.

This volume is a translation of a work originally published in German in 1965/66. Eichrodt's moderately critical approach in the main agrees with the biblical presentation of Ezekiel and his ministry. Eichrodt applies a critical methodology that he believes does reveal some non-Ezekiel passages, but what is left, in his opinion, is without a doubt original. S★★★

Greenberg, M. *Ezekiel 1–20*. AB. Doubleday, 1983. *Ezekiel 21–37*. AB. Doubleday, 1997. xv/388 pp. and 371 pp.

This is a very interesting commentary on the Book of Ezekiel. Greenberg is well-aware of what he is trying to accomplish as a commentator (see *Ezekiel 1–20*, 18–27). He advocates what he calls a holistic approach, which basically treats the MT as it stands and as a whole. Very stimulating. MS★★★★

Hals, R. M. *Ezekiel*. FOTL. Eerdmans, 1989. xiii/363 pp.

Well-researched and well-written, but definitely, like the series as a whole, geared to scholars. If ministers or students delve into this book, the most helpful sections will be those concerning bibliography, structure, and intention. S★★★★

Stuart, D. *Ezekiel*. CC. Word, 1989. 426 pp.

Stuart is one of the few professional academics asked to contribute to this series. His volume has a slightly different flavor than the others. It has more actual interpretation and explanation of the text and fewer personal anecdotes. Stuart's writing style is nevertheless quite engaging. LM****

Taylor, J. B. *Ezekiel*. TOTC. Inter-Varsity, 1969. 285 pp.

This commentary is especially designed for those who know little about Ezekiel. It is conservative and easy to read. LM**

Wevers, J. W. *Ezekiel*. NCB. Sheffield/Marshall Pickering, 1969. x/355 pp.

Wevers presents a more traditional critical approach than Greenberg and is a lot less stimulating than other critical scholars, especially Zimmerli. S**

Zimmerli, W. *Ezekiel*. 2 vols. Hermeneia. Fortress/SCM, 1979, 1982. xlvi/509 pp. and xxxiv/606 pp.

The German original was published in 1969. An English translation was long anticipated because of Zimmerli's breadth of knowledge and incredible insight. Zimmerli represents the best of critical thought on the Book of Ezekiel. MS*****

Daniel

Anderson, R. A. *Signs and Wonders: A Commentary on the Book of Daniel*. ITC. Handsel, 1984. xvii/158 pp.

This is a competent, well-written popularization of certain critical theories about Daniel. LM***

Baldwin, J. G. *Daniel*. TOTC. Inter-Varsity, 1978. 210 pp.

Although short, this commentary contains a wealth of information and careful exegetical insight. Baldwin is a balanced and sane exegete, which is important to note in a commentary on a book that attracts some wild ideas. Baldwin is solidly conservative, but not rigid. LM****

Collins, J. J. *Daniel.* FOTL. Eerdmans, 1984. xii/120 pp.

A very competent form-critical analysis and summary of discussion of Daniel. The book is technical and for that reason will only really interest scholars. S****

Collins, J. J. *Daniel.* Hermeneia. Fortress, 1993. 498 pp.

The lengthy and extremely informative introduction includes an essay by A. Y. Collins, "The Influence of Daniel on the New Testament." J. J. Collins is a noted Daniel expert, and this volume is the apex of his decades-long research. It is critical in its approach, but evangelicals can learn much from this volume. MS*****

Ferguson, S. B. *Daniel.* CC. Word, 1988. 252 pp.

Ferguson provides a good balance of exposition and application. His narrative is spiced with helpful illustrations and anecdotes. He avoids speculation on some of the prophecies, preferring to concentrate on the theme of the "good news of the kingdom of God." Good christological focus. LM****

Goldingay, J. *Daniel.* WBC. Nelson/Paternoster, 1989. liii/351 pp.

Goldingay's is perhaps the most comprehensive commentary on Daniel listed here. He gives insight into historical, literary, and theological issues concerning the book. He also demonstrates an amazing grasp of the secondary literature. Many of his readers will be put off by some of his radical (at least for an evangelical) conclusions, most notable of which are that the stories in chapters 1–6 are fictitious and the visions are quasi-prophecies. However, it would be a major mistake to ignore this important commentary while studying Daniel. MS*****

Hartman, L. F., and A. A. Dilella. *The Book of Daniel.* AB. Doubleday, 1978. xiv/345 pp.

This is one of the skimpier volumes in the Anchor Bible series. It takes a typically critical approach to the date of the book. The exegetical comments are not that helpful. S*

Heaton, E. *Daniel.* TBC. SCM, 1956. 251 pp.

In his lengthy introduction, Heaton draws a close connection between the author of Daniel and Ben Sira, as well as the Hasideans. He argues that Daniel should be identified with the Danel of Ugaritic literature. He presents a typical argument for the late date of the book. Nonetheless, it may still be profitably read. LM★★★★

Lacocque, A. *The Book of Daniel.* John Knox/SPCK, 1979. xxvi/302 pp.

This is an English translation of a French commentary originally published in 1976. Although he does provide some helpful textual and philological notes, Lacocque is strong on theology and contemporary application (at least relatively so for a critical scholar). He adopts a traditional critical dating and interpretation. MS★★★

Longman, Tremper, III. *Daniel.* NIVAC. Zondervan/Hodder & Stoughton, 1999. 313 pp.

In keeping with the design of the NIVAC series, I explore the original meaning and contemporary significance of this interesting, yet often enigmatic biblical book. In addition, I explain how I move from the ancient text to our modern situation. Daniel becomes, in the first six chapters, a study of how a person of faith not only copes but thrives in a hostile cultural setting. In the last half of the book, it raises the question of how we are to understand the apocalyptic sections of Scripture that describe the end of history. The theme of the whole book is that "in spite of present difficult circumstances, God is in control and will defeat the forces of evil and oppression." LM

Lucas, E. C. *Daniel.* Apollos Old Testament Commentary. Inter-Varsity, 2002. 359 pp.

Lucas is sensitive to Daniel as literature and theology. He provides a special study of the ancient Near Eastern background to the imagery in chapters 7–12. Many, however, including myself, will find his arguments in favor of a second-century date for the book weak, though he does argue in a way that is consistent with a high view of biblical authority. MS***

Miller, S. M. *Daniel.* NAC. Broadman, 1994. 348 pp.

Miller writes competently in defense of a conservative approach to the book. He concentrates on historical issues and the basic theological message. In the apocalyptic sections, he adopts a literal (plain) reading of the text. LM***

Montgomery, J. A. *Daniel.* ICC. T & T Clark, 1927. xxxi/488 pp.

This commentary concentrates on the building blocks of exegesis like philology and text. It becomes the basis for the theological comments of more recent commentaries as diverse as Young and Porteous. S****

Porteous, N. W. *Daniel.* OTL. Westminster/SCM, 1965. 173 pp.

Porteous concentrates on theology, not language. The commentary is short. Porteous adopts a critical stance toward the book. S**

Russell, D. S. *Daniel.* DSB. Westminster, 1981. 244 pp.

Russell is one of the previous generation's leading critical interpreters of apocalyptic literature. In his introduction, he dates the book late and gives a very unsatisfactory explanation of pseudonymity. However, his insistence on the present relevance of the book (over against a speculative futuristic approach) has much to commend itself. LM***

Towner, W. S. *Daniel.* Interp. John Knox, 1984. xi/186 pp.

This commentary concentrates on the theology of the book and is written from a critical perspective. The writing is clear and often insightful. MS***

Wallace, R. S. *The Lord Is King: The Message of Daniel.* BST. Inter-Varsity, 1979. 200 pp.

Wallace has written a good, popular exposition from an evangelical perspective. Solid research backs up his comments. The introduction provides a helpful conservative defense against a late dating of the book. LM****

Young, E. J. *The Prophecy of Daniel.* Banner of Truth, 1949. 330 pp.

The importance of this commentary is found in its firm and intelligent conservative stance. Young polemicizes against critical and dispensationalist approaches. He is not particularly sensitive to the literary nature or biblical theology of the book, but he is an excellent language scholar. MS***

Hosea

Achtemeier, E. *Minor Prophets I.* NIBCOT. Hendrickson/ Paternoster, 1996. 390 pp.

Achtemeier produces a good, solid, but not particularly exciting exegesis of the Minor Prophets through Micah. LM***

Andersen, F. I., and D. N. Freedman. *Hosea.* AB. Doubleday, 1980. xvii/701 pp.

This massive commentary is one of the best on any biblical book. For one thing, the authors are permitted the space to do a fuller job of commenting on the Hebrew text. Both authors are well-known, respected linguists. Andersen has some theological sense. The book is marred a little by a syllable-counting approach to meter. MS*****

Beeby, H. D. *Hosea: Grace Abounding.* ITC. Handsel, 1989. x/189 pp.

Proportionately, this is one of the more substantial commentaries in the series. Beeby gives some helpful clues in the introduction to using his commentary. He reads the text as a Christian in a refreshing way. LM***

Craigie, P. C. *Twelve Prophets.* 2 vols. DSB. Westminster, 1985. ix/239 pp.

As in most series, the Minor Prophets get short shrift in terms of space. This does not mean that the present commentary is worthless; Craigie is too insightful for that. It is only that it could be so much better if twice as many pages were allocated to the Minor Prophets. LM***

Garrett, D. A. *Hosea, Joel.* NAC. Broadman, 1997. 426 pp.

See under Joel.

Harper, W. R. *Amos and Hosea.* ICC. T & T Clark, 1905. clxxxi/424 pp.

Harper is very concerned to separate what he considers to be "authentic" Amos materials from later additions. He uses obsolete poetical criteria for emendation. In the introduction he places Amos and Hosea in a critically reconstructed history of prophetism, and gives a history of the composition of biblical literature. S***

Hubbard, D. A. *Hosea.* TOTC. Inter-Varsity, 1989. 234 pp.

Hubbard's commentary on Hosea is proportionately one of the most extensive in the series. His commentary on the fourteen chapters of Hosea is nearly as long as Baldwin's on 1 and 2 Samuel. Hubbard takes full advantage of this fact to provide a compellingly written, thoughtful analysis of Hosea's prophecy. Hosea is one of the more difficult books of the Bible to interpret. His commentary is based on sound scholarship and extensive research, and is extremely readable. LM****

Kidner, D. *The Message of Hosea: Love to the Loveless.* BST. Inter-Varsity, 1981. 142 pp.

This volume is one of the most engaging in the series. Kidner, with his usual skill, combines scholarship, pastoral insight, and concern with a vital writing style. LM****

Limburg, J. *Hosea–Micah.* Interp. John Knox, 1988. xi/201 pp.

This readable commentary concentrates on themes in selected texts. Brief, but very stimulating. LM***

Mays, J. L. *Hosea.* OTL. Westminster/SCM, 1969. x/190 pp.

Mays concentrates on the theological meaning of the text to the subordination of philology, text, and other exegetical concerns. He comes from a moderately critical perspective. MS***

McComiskey, T. "Hosea." In *The Minor Prophets: An Exegetical and Expository Commentary.* Ed. T. McComiskey. Vol. 1. Baker, 1992.

For serious study of Hosea, this commentary is a must. The volume offers both close reading of the Hebrew and a separate exposition of the book. An important commentary for those who preach on the book. Also included in this volume are commentaries on Joel by R. B. Dillard, and J. Niehaus on Amos (see under those books). MS*****

McKeating, H. *Amos, Hosea, Micah.* CBC. Cambridge University Press, 1971. x/198 pp.

McKeating ably sets the eighth-century background to these three prophets. He takes a moderately critical approach, but is engaging and informative. LM****

Smith, G. V. *Hosea/Amos/Micah.* NIVAC. Zondervan/ Hodder & Stoughton, 2001. 596 pp.

See under Amos.

Stuart, D. *Hosea–Jonah.* WBC. Nelson/Paternoster, 1987. xlv/537 pp.

This is one of the best recent commentaries on the Minor Prophets. It is a must-buy for everyone preaching on these books. It is intelligently conservative and emphasizes theology without ignoring the other aspects of the text. Shows how these prophets operated in a tradition going back to the covenant curses of the Pentateuch. MS★★★★

Wolff, H. W. *Hosea.* Hermeneia. Fortress/SCM, 1974. xxiii/259 pp.

Originally published in German in 1965, Wolff's work on Hosea has been the most influential force in Hosea studies for more than two decades. This is an excellent commentary on all aspects of the text and is written from a critical perspective. MS★★★★

Joel

Achtemeier, E. *Minor Prophets I.* NIBCOT. Hendrickson/Paternoster, 1996. 390 pp.

See under Hosea.

Allen, L. C. *Joel, Obadiah, Jonah, and Micah.* NICOT. Eerdmans, 1976. 427 pp.

See under Jonah.

Barton, J. *Joel and Obadiah.* OTL. Westminster John Knox, 2001. xxi/168 pp.

See also under Obadiah. He dates Joel to the early Second Temple, but the second half of Joel may be later. MS★★★★

Craigie, P. C. *Twelve Prophets.* 2 vols. DSB. Westminster, 1985. ix/239 pp.

See under Hosea.

Crenshaw, J. L. *Joel.* AB. Doubleday, 1995. 240 pp.

Crenshaw delivers an incisive commentary on the book, examining the literary nature as well as historical background and theological message. He questions whether Joel attributes the suffering of God's people to their sin, since the text nowhere makes this connection. However, the answer to the suffering is clear: Yahweh. MS★★★★

Dillard, R. B. "Joel." In *The Minor Prophets: An Exegetical and Expository Commentary.* Ed. T. McComiskey. Vol. 1. Baker, 1992.

Dillard has written a thoughtful and profound commentary on this intriguing biblical book. It combines an excellent technical investigation (philology, text, etc.) with an interesting theological study. If you get only one commentary on Joel, this should be it. MS*****

Finley, T. J. *Joel, Amos, Obadiah.* WEC. Moody, 1990. 417 pp.

This is a fully conceived commentary interested in all aspects of the biblical books that it studies. There are comments about history, literary matters, theology, philology, and practical application. Finley takes careful and reasoned positions. His writing style is clear and interesting. MS****

Garrett, D. A. *Hosea, Joel.* NAC. Broadman, 1997. 426 pp.

Garrett is a clear writer who reaches his exegetical conclusions in a reasoned manner and with appropriate restraint, qualities needed in the treatment of these two books whose study entails contact with many controversies. LM****

Hubbard, D. A. *Joel and Amos.* TOTC. Inter-Varsity, 1989. 245 pp.

This volume is brief, yet very useful—particularly in the areas of historical background, theology, and application. Well-written. LM****

Limburg, J. *Hosea–Micah.* Interp. John Knox, 1988. xi/201 pp.

See under Hosea.

Ogden, G. S., and R. R. Deutsch. *Joel and Malachi: A Promise of Hope, a Call to Obedience.* ITC. Handsel, 1987. x/120 pp.

These are competent, concise commentaries on two important Minor Prophets. Ogden and Deutsch appear to pay more attention to the contemporary relevance of the text—an announced intention of the series. LM***

Smith, J. M. P., W. H. Ward, and J. H. Bewer. *Micah, Zephaniah, Nahum, Habakkuk, Obadiah, and Joel.* ICC. T & T Clark, 1911. xix/537 pp.

See under Micah.

Stuart, D. *Hosea–Jonah.* WBC. Nelson/Paternoster, 1987. xlv/537 pp.

See under Hosea.

Watts, J. D. W. *The Books of Joel, Obadiah, Jonah, Nahum, Habakkuk, and Zephaniah.* CBC. Cambridge University Press, 1975. x/190 pp.

There are short, helpful introductions to each book. Watts explores the connection between these books and the day of the Lord and worship themes. He argues that these prophecies are prophetic liturgies. LM***

Wolff, H. W. *Joel and Amos.* Hermeneia. Fortress/SCM, 1977. xxiv/392 pp.

This commentary was written originally in German in 1969 and is a benchmark study of both books. Written from a moderately critical perspective. MS****

Amos

Achtemeier, E. *Minor Prophets I.* NIBCOT. Hendrickson/ Paternoster, 1996. 390 pp.

See under Hosea.

Andersen, F. I., and D. N. Freedman. *Amos.* AB. Doubleday, 1989. xliii/977 pp.

This massive commentary is obviously not for those who are only casually interested in the Book of Amos. The incredible detail is especially welcomed by the scholar as well as the seminary student and studious pastor. The authors are explicit about their method, and much can be carried over to the study of other biblical books. The commentary focuses on the final form of the text. It explains the changes in Amos's message by "dynamic developments in the prophet's career" rather than by a later editor who radically transforms his message. They do see evidence of editorial activity, but observe a "coherence between prophet and editor" (74). There is a lot of information in this commentary. It is a must for those who really want to delve into the Hebrew text of Amos. MS*****

Craigie, P. C. *Twelve Prophets.* DSB. 2 vols. Westminster, 1985. ix/239 pp.

See under Hosea.

Harper, W. R. *Amos and Hosea.* ICC. T & T Clark, 1905. clxxxi/424 pp.

See under Hosea.

Hubbard, D. A. *Joel and Amos.* TOTC. Inter-Varsity, 1989. 245 pp.

See under Joel.

Limburg, J. *Hosea–Micah.* Interp. John Knox, 1988. 201 pp.

See under Hosea.

Martin-Achard, R., and S. Paul Re'emi. *Amos and Lamentations: God's People in Crisis.* ITC. Handsel, 1984. viii/134 pp.

Martin-Achard concentrates on exposition and social application. LM***

Mays, J. L. *Amos.* OTL. Westminster/SCM, 1969. 176 pp.

Mays provides an extensive treatment of the book from a moderately critical perspective. He presents philological and other technical analyses, but does not lose sight of the theological message of the book. MS****

McKeating, H. *Amos, Hosea, Micah.* CBC. Cambridge University Press, 1971. x/198 pp.

See under Hosea.

Motyer, J. A. *Amos: The Day of the Lion.* BST. Inter-Varsity, 1974. 208 pp.

This volume, one of the first in the series, is well-written by a competent and popular expositor. Although popular, the volume does have substantial research behind it. LM***

Niehaus, J. "Amos." In *The Minor Prophets: An Exegetical and Expository Commentary.* Ed. T. McComiskey. Vol. 1. Baker, 1992.

The strength of this commentary is in its sensitivity to historical background and reference. This approach is aided by the author's competence in archaeology and ancient Near Eastern studies. The concept of covenant is fully exposed in relationship to this eighth-century prophet. MS****

Paul, S. M. *Amos.* Hermeneia. Fortress, 1991. xxvii/406 pp.

This is the second Amos commentary in the series (see Wolff). Paul's commentary is to be preferred for its interest in the text's integrity. As opposed to Wolff, who posits six redactional layers to the book, Paul ascribes virtually the whole book to Amos. He writes clearly, and his work is extremely well-researched. MS*****

Smith, B. K. "Amos." Pp. 23–170 in *Amos, Obadiah, Jonah.* NAC. Broadman, 1995.

A competent commentary with a clear introduction to the historical background of the book. LM***

Smith, G. V. *Amos: A Commentary.* 2d ed. Mentor Commentaries. Christian Focus, 1998. 398 pp.

Smith has produced a magisterial treatment of the Book of Amos from an evangelical perspective. He exegetes the text with extensive treatment of text, philology, literary structure, and theological message. MS****

Smith, G. V. *Hosea/Amos/Micah.* NIVAC. Zondervan/ Hodder & Stoughton, 2001. 596 pp.

Smith has already written one of the most extensive scholarly treatments of the original meaning of the Book of Amos. It is in the area of original meaning of all three of these early prophets that he is strongest. The sections on contemporary significance are often helpful, but not quite as strong as in some of the other volumes of this series. LM***

Stuart, D. *Hosea–Jonah.* WBC. Nelson/Paternoster, 1987. xlv/537 pp.

See under Hosea.

Vawter, B. *Amos, Hosea, Micah, with an Introduction to Classical Poetry.* OTM. Michael Glazier, 1981. 169 pp.

This volume is a well-written and lucid presentation of three of the most prominent Minor Prophets and of prophecy in general. Written from a critical perspective. LM***

Wolff, H. W. *Joel and Amos.* Hermeneia. Fortress, 1977. xxiv/392 pp.

See under Joel.

Obadiah

Achtemeier, E. *Minor Prophets I.* NIBCOT. Hendrickson/ Paternoster, 1996. 390 pp.

See under Hosea.

Allen, L. C. *Joel, Obadiah, Jonah, and Micah.* NICOT. Eerdmans, 1976. 427 pp.

See under Jonah.

Baker, D. W., T. D. Alexander, and B. K. Waltke. *Obadiah, Jonah, Micah.* TOTC. Inter-Varsity, 1988. 207 pp.

Baker wrote the section on Obadiah. He takes a highly competent, evangelical approach to the book, emphasizing historical background and theology. LM****

Barton, J. *Joel and Obadiah.* OTL. Westminster John Knox, 2001. 168 pp.

A very well-executed historical-critical commentary on these two Minor Prophets. Barton refuses to focus on the final form and wants to find the original setting, which will make this commentary less interesting to most, though he is an engaging writer. Dates the first part of Obadiah to the exile, but states that the second half is an eschatological addition. MS****

Coggins, R. J., and S. P. Re'emi. *Nahum, Obadiah, Esther: Israel among the Nations.* ITC. Handsel, 1985. x/140 pp.

These three books are presented as expressions of late attitudes toward the Gentile nations. The authors provide a competent interpretation from a moderately critical perspective. LM***

Craigie, P. C. *Twelve Prophets.* 2 vols. DSB. Westminster, 1985. ix/239 pp.

See under Hosea.

Eaton, J. H. *Obadiah, Nahum, Habakkuk, Zephaniah.* TBC. SCM, 1961. 159 pp.

Eaton identifies these prophets with temple service. He writes well and knowledgeably. LM***

Limburg, J. *Hosea–Micah.* Interp. John Knox, 1988. 201 pp.

See under Hosea.

Niehaus, J. "Obadiah." In *The Minor Prophets: An Exegetical and Expository Commentary.* Ed. T. McComiskey. Vol. 2. Baker, 1993.

Niehaus gives us one of the most extensive treatments of this short book. He combines historical, literary, and theological insight in this helpful commentary. He is open to the position that the author is the same person who plays an important role in the Elijah–Ahab narrative (1 Kings 18:1). LM★★★★

Raabe, P. R. *Obadiah.* AB. Doubleday, 1996. xxvi/310 pp.

This is an excellent commentary on the smallest book of the Old Testament. It is very thorough in discussion of words, historical issues, literary forms, and controversies. It deals with the meaning of the text, but not too extensively with its canonical significance. MS★★★★★

Smith, B. K. "Obadiah." In *Amos, Obadiah, Jonah.* NAC. Broadman, 1995. Pp. 171–201.

See under Amos. Not quite as strong as his contribution on Amos. Lacks detail and interest. LM★★★

Smith, J. M. P., W. H. Ward, and J. H. Bewer. *Micah, Zephaniah, Nahum, Habakkuk, Obadiah, and Joel.* ICC. T & T Clark, 1911. xix/537 pp.

See under Micah.

Stuart, D. *Hosea–Jonah.* WBC. Nelson/Paternoster, 1987. xlv/537 pp.

See under Hosea.

Watts, J. D. W. *The Books of Joel, Obadiah, Jonah, Nahum, Habakkuk, and Zephaniah.* CBC. Cambridge University Press, 1975. x/190 pp.

See under Joel.

Wolff, H. W. *Obadiah and Jonah.* Continental Commentary. Fortress, 1986. 191 pp.

See under Jonah.

Jonah

Achtemeier, E. *Minor Prophets I.* NIBCOT. Hendrickson/ Paternoster, 1996. 390 pp.

See under Hosea.

Allen, L. C. *Obadiah, Joel, Jonah, and Micah.* NICOT. Eerdmans, 1976. 427 pp.

Allen provides an up-to-date, insightful, and careful commentary on these interesting books. He writes with literary sensitivity, although many evangelicals will disagree with some of his conclusions. MS***

Baker, D. W., T. D. Alexander, and B. K. Waltke. *Obadiah, Jonah, Micah.* TOTC. Inter-Varsity, 1988. 207 pp.

See also under Obadiah and Micah. T. D. Alexander wrote the section on Jonah. Like the other authors in the book, Alexander provides a very helpful guide to the historical background and theology of the book. Alexander also provides a very interesting discussion of the genre of the book and concludes that it is didactic history writing. LM****

Baldwin, J. "Jonah." In *The Minor Prophets: An Exegetical and Expository Commentary.* Ed. T. McComiskey. Vol. 2. Baker, 1993.

Baldwin is always highly worth reading on any book on which she chooses to comment. In the case of Jonah, she is equaled by some others, but this is worthwhile. MS***

Craigie, P. C. *Twelve Prophets.* DSB. 2 vols. Westminster, 1985. ix/239 pp.

See under Hosea.

Knight, G. A. F., and F. W. Golka. *The Song of Songs and Jonah.* ITC. Handsel, 1988. ix/136 pp.

See under Song of Songs.

Limburg, J. *Jonah.* OTL. Westminster John Knox/SCM, 1993. 144 pp.

This book is a fine summary statement of a moderate critical analysis of the literary and theological dimensions of the Book of Jonah. It is well-written with interesting comments about the use of the book in the New

Testament, later Judaism and Islam, as well as on music and art. MS****

Mitchell, H. G., J. M. P. Smith, and J. A. Bewer. *Haggai, Zechariah, Malachi, and Jonah.* ICC. T & T Clark, 1912. xxvi/362 + 88 + 265 pp.

These are three volumes bound in one. All three authors provide classical critical studies of the most thorough kind. Technical and somewhat obsolete. S***

Page, F. S. "Jonah." Pp. 203–88 in *Amos, Obadiah, Jonah.* NAC. Broadman, 1995.

The introduction, among other things, presents a strong, well-argued case for taking the Book of Jonah as a historical, not fictional, work. Page also brings forward the best insights into the literary quality of the book. LM***

Sasson, J. M. *Jonah.* AB. Doubleday, 1990. xvi/368 pp.

This provocative commentary on the literary gem Jonah is well worth adding to a reference library. It not only rehearses previous views, but suggestively presents its own reading of the book. MS*****

Stuart, D. *Hosea–Jonah.* WBC. Nelson/Paternoster, 1987. xlv/537 pp.

See under Hosea.

Watts, J. D. W. *The Books of Joel, Obadiah, Jonah, Nahum, Habakkuk, and Zephaniah.* CBC. Cambridge University Press, 1975. x/190 pp.

See under Joel.

Wolff, H. W. *Obadiah and Jonah.* Continental Commentary. Fortress, 1986. 191 pp.

Wolff combines excellent philological ability with theological insight to produce a very helpful commentary on these two prophetic books. His stance is moderately critical. The format of the commentary makes his comments easy to get at. Good textual criticism. MS****

Micah

Achtemeier, E. *Minor Prophets I.* NIBCOT. Hendrickson/ Paternoster, 1996. 390 pp.

See under Hosea.

Alfaro, J. *Micah: Justice and Loyalty.* ITC. Handsel, 1989. x/85 pp.

In keeping with the purposes of the series, Alfaro provides a third-world reading of the prophet. He connects contemporary concerns about justice with the prophet's burning condemnation of the corrupt practices of his time. Moderately critical, this commentary, although brief, deserves reading because it provides a perspective to which many of us are oblivious. LM***

Allen, L. C. *Joel, Obadiah, Jonah, and Micah.* NICOT. Eerdmans, 1976. 427 pp.

See under Jonah.

Andersen, F. I., and D. N. Freedman. *Micah.* AB. Doubleday, 2000. 637 pp.

As one can tell from the length, this is the fullest treatment of the Book of Micah in recent times. The authors, both senior members of the guild of Old Testament studies, have thoroughly researched the book and also canvassed the secondary literature. The exegetical conclusions are not always satisfying, and the authors have little interest in broader theological issues, but for what it is, it is excellent. LM****

Baker, D. W., T. D. Alexander, and B. K. Waltke. *Obadiah, Jonah, Micah.* TOTC. Inter-Varsity, 1988. 207 pp.

See also under Obadiah and Jonah. Waltke wrote the section on Micah. It is the distillation of careful scholarship presented in an engaging format for the lay reader. LM*****

Barker, K. L. "Micah." Pp. 21–136 in *Micah/Nahum/Habakkuk/Zephaniah.* NAC. Broadman, 1999.

Good, competent commentary written from a premillennial perspective. However, the depth of research as indicated by the footnotes looks a bit dated. LM***

ben Zvi, Ehud. *Micah.* FOTL. Eerdmans, 2000. xvi/189 pp.

Ben Zvi has produced the most comprehensive analysis of the form-critical nature of the prophet. He has some very interesting comments to make on the fact that Micah is a book that is constantly reread. Even those who will not accept the conclusions of his analysis, and many evangelicals will not, will still find this commentary a useful compendium of other people's opinions. MS****

Craigie, P. C. *Twelve Prophets.* 2 vols. DSB. Westminster, 1985. ix/239 pp.

See under Hosea.

Hillers, D. R. *Micah.* Hermeneia. Fortress/SCM, 1984. xviii/192 pp.

Hillers avoids redaction criticism as too speculative. He approaches the book as a whole rather than diachronically. He sees Micah's oracles as a part of a "revitalization" program. This program protests oppression and looks to a new age. Should be consulted by serious students. MS***

Limburg, J. *Hosea–Micah.* Interp. John Knox, 1988. 201 pp.

See under Hosea.

Mays, J. L. *Micah.* OTL. Westminster/SCM, 1976. xii/169 pp.

A rare one-volume commentary on Micah. This is a well-written commentary that deserves close attention. Mays is a good scholar in the critical school. He communicates well and provides a well-rounded commentary. MS***

McKeating, H. *Amos, Hosea, Micah.* CBC. Cambridge University Press, 1971. x/198 pp.

See under Hosea.

Smith, G. V. *Hosea/Amos/Micah*. NIVAC. Zondervan/ Hodder & Stoughton, 2001. 596 pp.

See under Amos.

Smith, J. M. P., W. H. Ward, and J. H. Bewer. *Micah, Zeph-aniah, Nahum, Habakkuk, Obadiah, and Joel*. ICC. T & T Clark, 1911. xix/537 pp.

These authors are clear in their writing and critical in their approach to these Minor Prophets. They give a detailed overview to historical background. Technical and dated. S***

Smith, R. L. *Micah–Malachi*. WBC. Nelson/Paternoster, 1984. xvii/358 pp.

This commentary is solid and competent. It is hampered by size restrictions. The section on Nahum, for example, is extremely scanty and not particularly original. LM**

Waltke, B. "Micah." In *The Minor Prophets: An Exegetical and Expository Commentary*. Ed. T. McComiskey. Vol. 2. Baker, 1993.

This is a fuller form of Waltke's Tyndale commentary and is the best volume on the book. The author comments on all aspects of the book. MS*****

Nahum

Achtemeier, E. *Nahum–Malachi*. Interp. John Knox, 1986. x/201 pp.

An insightful commentary from a moderately critical perspective. LM***

Bailey, W. "Nahum." Pp. 137–243 in *Micah/Nahum/Ha-bakkuk/Zephaniah*. NAC. Broadman, 1999.

A strongly written, well-thought-out, and well-researched analysis of Nahum. Sensitive to the important theological themes. LM****

Baker, D. W. *Nahum, Habakkuk, and Zephaniah*. TOTC. Inter-Varsity, 1988. 121 pp.

Baker's commentary shares the strengths of the series: engaging writing style and emphasis on theology and historical background. LM****

Boadt, L. *Jeremiah 26–52, Habakkuk, Zephaniah, Nahum.* OTM. Michael Glazier, 1982. xxviii/213 pp.

See under Jeremiah.

Coggins, R. J., and S. P. Re'emi. *Nahum, Obadiah, Esther: Israel among the Nations.* ITC. Handsel, 1985. x/140 pp.

See under Obadiah.

Craigie, P. C. *Twelve Prophets.* 2 vols. DSB. Westminster, 1985. ix/239 pp.

See under Hosea.

Eaton, J. H. *Obadiah, Nahum, Habakkuk, Zephaniah.* TBC. SCM, 1961. 159 pp.

See under Obadiah.

Floyd, M. H. *Minor Prophets, Part 2.* FOTL. Eerdmans, 2000. xviii/641 pp.

An excellent form-critical study of these prophets, not only of the whole books but of their parts. Floyd does a better job than most connecting this narrow topic with the broader issues of interpretation. Nonetheless, this excellent work will only be helpful to scholars. S*****

Longman, T., III. "Nahum." In *The Minor Prophets: An Exegetical and Expository Commentary.* Ed. T. McComiskey. Vol. 2. Baker, 1993.

It would be inappropriate for me to comment, but then again you can guess my feelings on this commentary. I wouldn't have published it if I didn't like it! This volume shows the relevance of the book for today by explicating the theme of God as a warrior. MS

Maier, W. A. *The Book of Nahum.* Concordia, 1959. 386 pp.

This massive commentary on the short Book of Nahum was written by a radio preacher from the Lutheran Church–Missouri Synod. While knowledgeable in matters concerning the Old Testament, Maier adopts unnecessarily polemical and rigidly conservative positions in the exegesis of the text—including some outlandish attempts to preserve the Masoretic Text. The commentary contains a lot of information and raises the main issues of the book. It fails to provide the answers. LM***

Patterson, R. "Nahum." In *Nahum, Habakkuk, Zephaniah.* WEC. Moody, 1991.

Patterson shows tremendous literary sensitivity to Nahum. He also places the book in its historical context. He falls short in the theology of the book by emphasizing God's sovereignty, but not adequately discussing the divine warrior theme. MS****

Roberts, J. J. M. *Nahum, Habakkuk, and Zephaniah.* OTL. Westminster, 1991. 223 pp.

This commentary is another helpful addition to the study of these three Minor Prophets. There are extensive text-critical and philological notes, written in a way that even interested nonspecialists can understand. Roberts is more optimistic than most these days about the benefits of historical criticism. MS****

Robertson, O. P. *The Books of Nahum, Habakkuk, and Zephaniah.* NICOT. Eerdmans, 1990. x/357 pp.

This commentary gives significant attention to three of the more interesting, but often neglected, Minor Prophets. Robertson excels in theological analysis and pastoral application. The commentary is weak in philological and other technical studies. LM****

Smith, J. M. P., W. H. Ward, and J. H. Bewer. *Micah, Zephaniah, Nahum, Habakkuk, Obadiah, and Joel.* ICC. T & T Clark, 1911. xix/537 pp.

See under Micah.

Smith, R. L. *Micah–Malachi.* WBC. Nelson/Paternoster, 1984. xvii/358 pp.

See under Micah.

Watts, J. D. W. *The Books of Joel, Obadiah, Jonah, Nahum, Habakkuk, and Zephaniah.* CBC. Cambridge University Press, 1975. x/190 pp.

See under Joel.

Habakkuk

Achtemeier, E. *Nahum–Malachi.* Interp. John Knox, 1986. x/201 pp.

See under Nahum.

Andersen, F. I. *Habakkuk.* AB. Doubleday, 2001. xxii/387 pp.

Andersen has produced an excellent scholarly reading of the prophet Habakkuk. In his preface he expresses the desire to communicate with the nontechnical reader, and he indeed is a very clear writer. However, the depth of his analysis and the choice of his topics make this commentary better suited for the scholar and occasional minister. MS★★★★

Bailey, W. "Habakkuk." Pp. 245–378 in *Micah/Nahum/ Habakkuk/Zephaniah.* NAC. Holman, 1999.

See under Zephaniah.

Baker, D. W. *Nahum, Habakkuk, and Zephaniah.* TOTC. Inter-Varsity, 1988. 121 pp.

See under Nahum.

Boadt, L. *Jeremiah 26–52, Habakkuk, Zephaniah, Nahum.* OTM. Michael Glazier, 1982. xxviii/213 pp.

See under Jeremiah.

Bruce, F. F. "Habakkuk." In *The Minor Prophets: An Exegetical and Expository Commentary.* Ed. T. McComiskey. Vol. 2. Baker, 1993.

Normally identified as a New Testament scholar, the erudite Bruce is also highly competent on this Old Testament subject. MS***

Craigie, P. C. *Twelve Prophets.* 2 vols. DSB. Westminster, 1985. ix/239 pp.

See under Hosea.

Eaton, J. H. *Obadiah, Nahum, Habakkuk, Zephaniah.* TBC. SCM, 1961. 159 pp.

See under Obadiah.

Floyd, M. H. *Minor Prophets, Part 2.* FOTL. Eerdmans, 2000. xviii/641 pp.

See under Nahum.

Patterson, R. "Habakkuk." In *Nahum, Habakkuk, Zephaniah.* WEC. Moody, 1991.

See under Nahum. This commentary may be the best, in terms of quantity as well as quality of insight, on this Minor Prophet. It is particularly strong on literary and historical analysis. It is also helpful in its comments on theology, but would have benefited from a stronger sense of the divine warrior theme. MS****

Robertson, O. P. *The Books of Nahum, Habakkuk, and Zephaniah.* NICOT. Eerdmans, 1990. x/357 pp.

See under Nahum.

Smith, J. M. P., W. H. Ward, and J. H. Bewer. *Micah, Zephaniah, Nahum, Habakkuk, Obadiah, and Joel.* ICC. T & T Clark, 1911. xix/537 pp.

See under Micah.

Smith, R. L. *Micah–Malachi.* WBC. Nelson/Paternoster, 1984. xvii/358 pp.

See under Micah.

Szeles, M. E. *Habakkuk and Zephaniah: Wrath and Mercy.* ITC. Handsel, 1987. x/118 pp.

A helpful, competent study by a Romanian scholar. Unfortunately, she does not interact with her own society that much. She does set the books within their historical context. LM***

Zephaniah

Achtemeier, E. *Nahum–Malachi*. Interp. John Knox, 1986. x/201 pp.

See under Nahum.

Bailey, W. "Zephaniah." Pp. 379–505 in *Micah/Nahum/ Habakkuk/Zephaniah*. NAC. Holman, 1999.

Good solid commentary. The introduction tends to spend a lot of time describing (rather than substantially critiquing) other viewpoints on controversial issues, but the reader still gets Bailey's own views. LM***

Baker, D. W. *Nahum, Habakkuk, and Zephaniah*. TOTC. Inter-Varsity, 1988. 121 pp.

See under Nahum.

Berlin, A. *Zephaniah*. AB. Doubleday, 1994. xvi/165 pp.

Berlin is known as an exceptional practitioner of the literary method, and she does not disappoint us in this commentary, which shows great sensitivity to such issues as intertextuality. She also helpfully discusses text, semantics, historical issues, and theological message. MS*****

Craigie, P. C. *Twelve Prophets*. 2 vols. DSB. Westminster, 1985. ix/239 pp.

See under Hosea.

Eaton, J. H. *Obadiah, Nahum, Habakkuk, Zephaniah*. TBC. SCM, 1961. 159 pp.

See under Obadiah.

Floyd, M. H. *Minor Prophets, Part 2*. FOTL. Eerdmans, 2000. xviii/641 pp.

See under Nahum.

Motyer, J. A. "Zephaniah." In *The Minor Prophets: An Exegetical and Expository Commentary.* Ed. T. McComiskey. Vol. 3. Baker, 1998.

Motyer presents a readable and solid interpretation of Zephaniah. One of the more in-depth analyses. LM****

Patterson, R. "Zephaniah." In *Nahum, Habakkuk, Zephaniah.* WEC. Moody, 1991.

As in his work on Nahum and Habakkuk, Patterson does an excellent job on most aspects of the book. He is clear, engaging, and profound, particularly in areas of historical background and literary strategy. He does a good job on the theological message of the book, but an improvement could be made here. MS****

Robertson, O. P. *The Books of Nahum, Habakkuk, and Zephaniah.* NICOT. Eerdmans, 1990. x/357 pp.

See under Nahum.

Smith, J. M. P., W. H. Ward, and J. H. Bewer. *Micah, Zephaniah, Nahum, Habakkuk, Obadiah, and Joel.* ICC. T & T Clark, 1911. xix/537 pp.

See under Micah.

Smith, R. L. *Micah–Malachi.* WBC. Nelson/Paternoster, 1984. xvii/358 pp.

See under Micah.

Szeles, M. E. *Habakkuk and Zephaniah: Wrath and Mercy.* ITC. Handsel, 1987. x/118 pp.

See under Habakkuk.

Watts, J. D. W. *The Books of Joel, Obadiah, Jonah, Nahum, Habakkuk, and Zephaniah.* CBC. Cambridge University Press, 1975. x/190 pp.

See under Joel.

Haggai

Achtemeier, E. *Nahum–Malachi.* Interp. John Knox, 1986. x/201 pp.

See under Nahum.

Baldwin, J. G. *Haggai, Zechariah, Malachi.* TOTC. Inter-Varsity, 1972. 253 pp.

A very insightful, conservative commentary. LM***

Boadt, L. *Jeremiah 26–52, Habakkuk, Zephaniah, Nahum.* OTM. Michael Glazier, 1982. xxviii/213 pp.

See under Jeremiah.

Craigie, P. C. *Twelve Prophets.* 2 vols. DSB. Westminster, 1985. ix/239 pp.

See under Hosea.

Floyd, M. H. *Minor Prophets, Part 2.* FOTL. Eerdmans, 2000. xviii/641 pp.

See under Nahum.

Meyers, C. L., and E. M. Meyers. *Haggai; Zechariah 1–8.* AB. Doubleday, 1987. xcv/478 pp.

The Meyers treat Haggai and Zechariah 1–8 as not only stemming from the same period of time, but also as two parts of the same composite work. (They will treat the latter part of Zechariah in a subsequent commentary.) The Meyers are archaeologists, so their commentary is full of helpful historical and archaeological comments. The authors include an excellent bibliography. MS****

Mitchell, H. G., J. M. P. Smith, and J. A. Bewer. *Haggai, Zechariah, Malachi, and Jonah.* ICC. T & T Clark, 1912. xxvi/362 + 88 + 265 pp.

See under Jonah.

Motyer, J. A. "Haggai." In *The Minor Prophets: An Exegetical and Expository Commentary.* Ed. T. McComiskey. Vol. 3. Baker, 1998.

Good solid exposition, though very short. Motyer also has apologetic interests in the forefront as he counters various critical ideas. He is particularly adamant about Haggai having been his own editor. LM***

Petersen, D. L. *Haggai and Zechariah.* OTL. Westminster/SCM, 1984. 320 pp.

Petersen and the Meyers have much in common in their approach to the text. They are both critical in their understanding of historical questions, but neither gets bogged down completely in such issues. Petersen is more interested in a positive interpretation of the books than in exhaustive interaction with the secondary literature. Like the Meyers, he does an admirable job reconstructing the historical, sociological, archaeological, and economic background to the text. MS****

Redditt, P. L. *Haggai, Zechariah, Malachi.* NCB. Sheffield, 1995. 196 pp.

A short, readable commentary on these postexilic books. Redditt looks at the compositional history of these books in his introductions and provides historical background. The commentary proper focuses on the text itself. LM***

Smith, R. L. *Micah–Malachi.* WBC. Nelson/Paternoster, 1984. xvii/358 pp.

See under Micah.

Stuhlmueller, C. *Haggai and Zechariah.* ITC. Handsel, 1988. ix/165 pp.

This commentary is well-informed and written with flair. Stuhlmueller presents a moderately critical perspective that is concerned with present relevance. LM***

Verhoef, P. A. *The Books of Haggai and Malachi.* NICOT. Eerdmans, 1987. 384 pp.

Verhoef is a South African scholar who is considerably at home in postexilic literature. He does a careful job of exegeting the Hebrew text. He also explores the theological message of Haggai and Malachi and traces their themes into the New Testament. This commentary is more academic in style than many others in the NICOT series; thus, it is highly recommended as a scholarly guide to both of these prophetic books. MS***

Wolff, H. W. *Haggai.* Continental Commentary. Fortress, 1988. 128 pp.

Wolff, as usual, is clear, concise, and insightful. He sees Haggai as a "model of communication." After all, Haggai was the one who got the Israelites to rebuild the temple. Analyzes the book as the result of three "growth rings": Haggai's proclamation, the work of a Haggai chronicler, and interpolations. MS****

Zechariah

Achtemeier, E. *Nahum–Malachi.* Interp. John Knox, 1986. x/201 pp.

See under Nahum.

Baldwin, J. G. *Haggai, Zechariah, Malachi.* TOTC. Inter-Varsity, 1972.

See under Haggai.

Craigie, P. C. *Twelve Prophets.* 2 vols. DSB. Westminster, 1985. ix/239 pp.

See under Hosea.

Floyd, M. H. *Minor Prophets, Part 2.* FOTL. Eerdmans, 2000. xviii/641 pp.

See under Nahum.

McComiskey, T. "Zechariah." In *The Minor Prophets: An Exegetical and Expository Commentary.* Ed. T. McComiskey. Vol. 3. Baker, 1998.

McComiskey gives a very reasonable and interesting exposition of the book from a conservative perspective. He recognizes the issues connected with seeing chapters 9–14 as not part of the original Zecharian composition, but resists simply cutting these chapters off. He is a sensitive reader of the literary images and a very competent linguist. LM****

Meyers, C. L., and E. M. Meyers. *Haggai; Zechariah 1–8.*
AB. Doubleday, 1987. *Zechariah 9–14.* AB. Doubleday,
1993. xcv/478 pp. and xxiii/552 pp.

The Anchor Bible really has done it right with the Minor
Prophets. They have apparently given the authors of all the
volumes considerable latitude in length, and the Meyers
have used their freedom with great success. This is a wonder-
fully written and researched commentary that I have found
extremely provocative and largely persuasive. MS*****

Mitchell, H. G., J. M. P. Smith, and J. A. Bewer. *Haggai,
Zechariah, Malachi, and Jonah.* ICC. T & T Clark, 1912.
xxvi/362 + 88 + 265 pp.

See under Jonah.

Petersen, D. L. *Zechariah 9–14 and Malachi.* OTL. Westminster John Knox, 1995. xxi/233 pp.

See under Malachi.

Redditt, P. L. *Haggai, Zechariah, Malachi.* NCB. Sheffield,
1995. 196 pp.

See under Haggai.

Smith, R. L. *Micah–Malachi.* WBC. Nelson/Paternoster,
1984. xvii/358 pp.

See under Micah.

Stuhlmueller, C. *Haggai and Zechariah.* ITC. Handsel,
1988. ix/165 pp.

See under Haggai.

Malachi

Achtemeier, E. *Nahum–Malachi.* Interp. John Knox, 1986.
x/201 pp.

See under Nahum.

Baldwin, J. G. *Haggai, Zechariah, Malachi.* TOTC. Inter-
Varsity, 1972.

See under Haggai.

Craigie, P. C. *Twelve Prophets.* 2 vols. DSB. Westminster, 1985. ix/239 pp.

See under Hosea.

Floyd, M. H. *Minor Prophets, Part 2.* FOTL. Eerdmans, 2000. xviii/641 pp.

See under Nahum.

Hill, A. E. *Malachi.* AB. Doubleday, 1998. xliii/436 pp.

Hill provides an extensive and excellent analysis of the introductory issues connected with this book. His exposition of the book itself is also of high quality. The lay reader is forewarned that his writing and approach are fairly technical, even for the series. This is also one of the few volumes in this series that takes seriously connections with the New Testament. MS****

Kaiser, W. C. *Malachi: God's Unchanging Love.* Baker, 1984. 171 pp.

A practical commentary that combines scholarly tidbits with pastoral concern. The volume illustrates principles found in the author's *Toward an Exegetical Theology.* An appendix on how to use commentaries is included. LM***

Mitchell, H. G., J. M. P. Smith, and J. A. Bewer. *Haggai, Zechariah, Malachi, and Jonah.* ICC. T & T Clark, 1912. xxvi/362 + 88 + 265 pp.

See under Jonah.

Ogden, G. S., and R. R. Deutsch. *Joel and Malachi: A Promise of Hope, a Call to Obedience.* ITC. Handsel, 1987. x/120 pp.

See under Joel.

Petersen, D. L. *Zechariah 9–14 and Malachi.* OTL. Westminster John Knox /SCM, 1995. xxi/233 pp.

Petersen treats these chapters as three different oracles, each initiated by the Hebrew word *massa'.* He dates all three of the oracles to the Persian period. He emphasizes historical background and sociological analysis. He also discusses at length form-critical and redaction-critical issues, but he is not strong on other types of literary analysis or theological contributions. S***

Redditt, P. L. *Haggai, Zechariah, Malachi.* NCB. Sheffield, 1995. 196 pp.

See under Haggai.

Smith, R. L. *Micah–Malachi.* WBC. Nelson/Paternoster, 1984. xvii/358 pp.

See under Micah.

Stuart, D. "Malachi." In *The Minor Prophets: An Exegetical and Expository Commentary.* Ed. T. McComiskey. Vol. 3. Baker, 1998.

This commentary is particularly good in connecting the prophet to covenant curses and blessings. It sometimes is overly apologetic, as when it argues against the possibility that Malachi stands for "my messenger" rather than being a proper name. LM***

Verhoef, P. A. *The Books of Haggai and Malachi.* NICOT. Eerdmans, 1987.

See under Haggai.

Appendix A

Five-Star Commentaries

The following commentaries received the highest ratings for each of the biblical books. These may not be the commentaries for you (for instance, they may be too technical or too critical), but they are the best because they accomplish their intentions from their own theological perspective most successfully.

Hamilton, V. P. *The Book of Genesis*. 2 vols. NICOT. Eerdmans, 1990, 1995. 522 pp. and 774 pp.

Waltke, B. K., and Cathi J. Fredricks. *Genesis*. Zondervan, 2001. 656 pp.

Wenham, G. J. *Genesis 1–15*. WBC. Nelson/Paternoster, 1987. *Genesis 16–50*. WBC. Nelson/Paternoster, 1994. liii/353 pp. and 555 pp.

Childs, B. S. *The Book of Exodus*. OTL. Westminster/SCM, 1974. xxv/659 pp.

Enns, P. *Exodus*. NIVAC. Zondervan/Hodder & Stoughton, 2000. 448 pp.

Hartley, J. E. *Leviticus*. WBC. Nelson/Paternoster, 1992. lxxiii/496 pp.

Milgrom, J. *Leviticus 1–16*. AB. Doubleday, 1991. *Leviticus 17–22*. AB. Doubleday, 2000. *Leviticus 23–27*. AB. Doubleday, 2001. xviii/1,163 pp., xvii/624 pp., and xxi/818 pp.

Wenham, G. J. *The Book of Leviticus.* NICOT. Eerdmans, 1979. xiii/362 pp.

Milgrom, J. *Numbers.* JPS Torah Commentary. Jewish Publication Society, 1990. lxi/520 pp.

Olson, D. T. *Numbers.* Interp. John Knox, 1996. 196 pp.

Weinfeld, M. *Deuteronomy 1–11.* AB. Doubleday, 1991. xiv/448 pp.

Hess, R. S. *Joshua.* TOTC. Inter-Varsity, 1996. 320 pp.

Block, D. I. *Judges, Ruth.* NAC. Broadman, 1999. 765 pp.

Bush, R. W. *Ruth/Esther.* WBC. Nelson/Paternoster, 1996. xiv/514 pp.

Hubbard, R. L., Jr. *The Book of Ruth.* NICOT. Eerdmans, 1988. xiv/317 pp.

Provan, I. W. *1 and 2 Kings.* NIBCOT. Hendrickson/Paternoster, 1995. xiv/306 pp.

Dillard, R. B. *II Chronicles.* WBC. Nelson/Paternoster, 1987. xxiii/323 pp.

Japhet, S. *I and II Chronicles.* OTL. Westminster John Knox/SCM, 1993. xxv/1,077 pp.

Williamson, H. G. M. *Ezra–Nehemiah.* WBC. Nelson/Paternoster, 1985. xix/428 pp.

Jobes, K. *Esther.* NIVAC. Zondervan/Hodder & Stoughton, 1999. 248 pp.

Clines, D. J. A. *Job 1–20.* WBC. Nelson/Paternoster, 1989. cxi/501 pp.

Mays, J. L. *Psalms.* Interp. John Knox, 1994. xvii/457 pp.

Van Gemeren, W. *Psalms.* EBC 5. Zondervan, 1991.

Fox, Michael V. *Proverbs 1–9.* AB. Doubleday, 2000. xix/474 pp.

Gledhill, T. *The Message of the Song of Songs: The Lyrics of Love.* Inter-Varsity, 1994. 254 pp.

Keel, O. *The Song of Songs.* Continental Commentary. Fortress, 1994. ix/308 pp.

Pope, M. H. *Song of Songs.* AB. Doubleday, 1977. xxi/743 pp.

Lundbom, J. R. *Jeremiah 1–20.* AB. Doubleday, 1999. 934 pp.

Dobbs-Allsopp, F. W. *Lamentations.* Interp. John Knox, 2002. xiv/159 pp.

Provan, I. *Lamentations.* NCB. Sheffield/Marshall Pickering, 1991. 134 pp.

Block, D. I. *The Book of Ezekiel 1–24.* NICOT. Eerdmans, 1997. *The Book of Ezekiel 25–48.* NICOT. Eerdmans, 1998. xxi/887 pp. and xxiii/826 pp.

Duguid, I. *Ezekiel.* NIVAC. Zondervan/Hodder & Stoughton, 1999. 568 pp.

Zimmerli, W. *Ezekiel.* 2 vols. Hermeneia. Fortress/SCM, 1979, 1982. xlvi/509 pp. and xxxiv/606 pp.

Collins, J. J. *Daniel.* Hermeneia. Fortress, 1993. 498 pp.

Goldingay, J. *Daniel.* WBC. Nelson/Paternoster, 1989. liii/351 pp.

Andersen, F. I., and D. N. Freedman. *Hosea.* AB. Doubleday, 1980. xvii/701 pp.

McComiskey, T. "Hosea." In *The Minor Prophets: An Exegetical and Expository Commentary.* Ed. T. McComiskey. Vol. 1. Baker, 1992.

Dillard, R. B. "Joel." In *The Minor Prophets: An Exegetical and Expository Commentary.* Ed. T. McComiskey. Vol. 1. Baker, 1992.

Andersen, F. I., and D. N. Freedman. *Amos.* AB. Doubleday, 1989. xliii/977 pp.

Paul, S. M. *Amos.* Hermeneia. Fortress, 1991. xxvii/406 pp.

Sasson, J. M. *Jonah.* AB. Doubleday, 1990. xvi/368 pp.

Baker, D. W., T. D. Alexander, and B. K. Waltke. *Obadiah, Jonah, Micah.* TOTC. Inter-Varsity, 1988. 207 pp.

Waltke, B. "Micah." In *The Minor Prophets: An Exegetical and Expository Commentary.* Ed. T. McComiskey. Vol. 2. Baker, 1993.

Author's note: Please note that my own commentaries are unrated and therefore not included in this list. For a listing of my commentaries, see Appendix B.

Appendix B

Commentaries by Tremper Longman III

Daniel. NIVAC. Zondervan/Hodder & Stoughton, 1999. 313 pp.

Ecclesiastes. NICOT. Eerdmans, 1998. xvi/306 pp.

"Nahum." In *The Minor Prophets: An Exegetical and Expository Commentary.* Ed. T. McComiskey. Vol. 2. Baker, 1993.

Song of Songs. NICOT. Eerdmans, 2001. xvi/238 pp.

Name Index

147